ME AND NU:
CHILDHOOD AT COOLE

ME AND NU:
CHILDHOOD AT COOLE

ANNE GREGORY

illustrated by
JOYCE DENNYS

with a prefatory note
by
MAURICE COLLIS

COLIN SMYTHE
Gerrards Cross

Printed in Great Britain
by The Guernsey Press Co. Ltd., Guernsey, C.I.. GY1 3BW

To Richard

PREFATORY NOTE

Me and Nu requires a prefatory note because it presupposes the knowledge of a few biographical facts, which the general reader will not possess.

The author, Anne Gregory, is the grand-daughter of Lady Gregory, Yeats' friend and colleague. Lady Gregory's name was Augusta Persse. She was born in 1852 at the Persse seat, Roxborough, in Galway. In 1880, aged 28 she married Sir William Gregory, who had retired from the Governorship of Ceylon. His residence and estate was called Coole Park. On her marriage to him, as Lady Gregory, she moved from Roxborough to Coole, a distance of about twenty miles. In 1881 she had a son, William Robert Gregory, usually known as Robert. In 1892 the marriage was ended by the death of Sir William, who was thirty-five years older than his wife. Left a widow at the age of thirty-nine, she remained at Coole until her death at the age of eighty in 1932. Between 1892 and 1932, a period of forty years, she became a friend and colleague of the poet Yeats and was one of the founders of the Abbey Theatre in Dublin, the pivot of the Irish Literary Movement. All its leading figures used to come and stay at Coole, which grew to be the most famous house in Ireland. Not only were the poet Yeats, his brother Jack Yeats, the artist, A.E., and such pillars of the Abbey Theatre as Douglas Hyde, founder of the Gaelic League, the playwrights O'Casey and Synge, constant visitors, but celebrities from outside the orbit of the Abbey Theatre like Bernard Shaw and Augustus John were to be met with there.

Lady Gregory was trustee of the Coole Estate on behalf of her son until he became of age. He lived at Coole with his mother and helped in Dublin at the Abbey. He married Margaret Graham Parry in 1907 and he, his wife and children would stay for much of the summer at a house called Mount Vernon on the Galway coast, which had been given to him by Lady Gregory as a wedding present.

Robert and his wife were more often than not away from Coole: they lived in Paris where they both did a great deal of painting, and at the beginning of the First World War they had a house in Royal Hospital Road, London. During the First World War Robert joined the Connaught Rangers and then the Royal Flying Corps.

Robert's three children were Richard, Anne and Catherine. All three were born and brought up at Coole and Anne and Catherine, nicknamed 'Nu', never left it until they went to school.

The narrative which follows here is Anne Gregory's recollection of what living at Coole with her grandmother was like. Her account is very cleverly constructed. One hears, as it were, the voice of a little girl of ten or twelve, though the voice of the writer, now a woman of middle age sounds in undertone. The elder voice murmurs, unobtrusively, so that the reader gets the double impression. There are many amusing passages. Something is added to what hitherto we have known of Shaw, Augustus John, Yeats and the rest. The stature of Lady Gregory is subtly increased. She was a wonderful woman and also a wonderful grandmother.

MAURICE COLLIS

8

CHAPTER I

". . . And Brer Rabbit he lay low and said nuffin' . . ."

Grandma put down 'Uncle Remus' in her lap, and laughed and laughed, tears poured down her face, and she dabbed at them with her pocket handkerchief.

My sister Nu and I were having competitions. Sitting on the floor in front of the library fire, we lighted larch twigs in the fire, and held them in the curly wrought-iron tops of the fire dogs, seeing whose twig would glow the longest.

"Oh Grandma, *please* don't stop—please read another story," we begged. "You can't stop now . . . it's not nearly bedtime." My voice anyway was tearful in its entreaty. I had lost the last two heats of the competition—bad wood, I had no doubt—and I was determined to establish my superiority over my young sister before bedtime.

Grandma dabbed her eyes again and—horror—draped her now very damp handkerchief over the top of *my* fire dog, where it began steaming at once like a kettle in the heat of the fire.

I sulked.

'Uncle Remus' was all right, but not nearly so amusing if you couldn't play 'Light out' at the same time. And it was very unfair that Nu could practise all the time on her dog.

As Grandma read, and apparently without taking her eyes from the book, she leant forward and turned her handkerchief round, now draping it over Nu's firedog . . .

It was heavenly in the library.

We always came in after tea in the winter, and sat in front of the enormous open fire, burning the great logs of beech, ash and fir cut daily by Mike and Paddy, and stacked by them in great baskets on either side of the fireplace.

Grandma was very good with fires, and when it burned slowly because there was too much beech, and looked a bit dull, she told us it was time to help it a bit. Beside the log basket there was a large brass box full of kippeens and fircones that Grandma used to collect as she went round the woods, or up and down to the gardens or yards.

It was tremendous fun tucking the kippeens under the logs, and choosing fircones with white tips of resin, that caught alight with a whish and a crackle, and blazed like small torches. The grey ash, that looked dead, was really quite warm, and the smoke from the kippeens rose quicker and quicker as though in a frenzy to get up the chimney, and suddenly the whole fire would catch alight and blaze with a very contented and deep sound. We learned a lot about wood from Grandma, who adored her woods and her trees. "Beech makes a lovely fire" she told

10

us, "very hot, but it is lost unless you have some warm ashes to help it get going. Ash is all right for a short while, but it burns brightly and is finished in no time at all, and chestnut pops a lot" . . . and we'd look at the logs burning in the grate, and see what had been put on, to make certain that we were going to have a warm fire without too many sparks jumping out on the carpet.

There was a very special smell in the library. The whole room was lined from ceiling to floor with books in old leather bindings. Our great great grandfather, Grandma told us, had been a great scholar and a great collector, and there were a lot of beautiful and valuable books there.

We used to creep in to the library surreptitiously now and then, and take one out of a shelf to look at. But we must have been unlucky, as they were indescribably dull. Sometimes we thought that perhaps the best must be at the top, and we'd climb to the top of the library steps to get one from near the ceiling, but we never found anything to interest us at all; nothing with coloured pictures or drawings or anything like that.

Sometimes on a very wet Sunday, Grandma would get out an enormous book, usually kept in a locked cupboard near the ground, and we'd look at Bible Illustrations in this, sitting on the floor, as it was too heavy to lift on to a table. I found these slightly frightening. I didn't at all like the pictures of a direct beam of light from a cloud, which shone on one person only, leaving everyone else in darkness; and Nu only wanted to look at one picture anyway—Absalom hanging by his hair from a tree.

The curtains added to the special smell in the library. We thought that they were rather dull old things, rather faded, but of course part of the library, and we were affronted when we got a terrific chiding for playing 'tig' in and out of them in the three windows. "Those were specially made and hand-painted for the tent of the Maharajah of Cawnpore at the Jubilee" Grandma told us, "and were given by him to your grandfather as a present as a special gesture of friendship. You really must treat them with more respect." We gave the curtains a sour look. How boring; and no more tig.

Grandma shut the book with a firm clap, and we knew that no entreaty, however heartfelt, would make her go on reading once the book had been shut like that.

Bed.

Anyway we couldn't play our game, because of the handkerchief, so it didn't matter so much . . . but it was a funny thing about 'Uncle Remus'; when Grandma read it it was such fun, and Brer Fox and Brer Rabbit sounded so sensible like real people, and talked quite clearly, yet one day when Grandma was away, I got hold of the book, and said that I would read it to Nu. I could make no sense of the book at all. I couldn't understand a single word; it was all quite extraordinary, not a single thing was the same as the book Grandma read to us; even the pictures on nearly every page seemed rather unfriendly when one couldn't understand the language under them. I put the book back feeling slightly guilty, as though I had caught Grandma out in a slight form of cheating.

Grandma read to us every evening. Fennimore Cooper's 'The Last of the Mohicans' was one of our favourites. 'Huckleberry Finn' and 'Tom Sawyer' were all right, but the horrible story of the cave and the bats was nearly unbearable, and I had horrid daymares about them, whenever we went near the caves in the Galway Avenue. 'Vice Versa' we thoroughly enjoyed, and 'Peep of Day' was Sunday reading, but 'Swiss Family Robinson' was our favourite.

'Swiss Family Robinson' was marvellous, and daily we tried to do what the family had done the night before. We were really very good at stalking wild duck on the edge of the lake with our bows and arrows. We never actually managed to kill one, but though our bows were very good, being made for us by Mike from a branch of Irish yew, the arrows were never very straight. They were made from slim ash saplings, and we were certain that the knots on the sides made the arrow fly off course. Then one birthday we were given 'real' bows and arrows, and with these we were certain that we could keep the house in game. I once hit a pigeon that I had stalked as it sat cooing like mad in a tree. It didn't fall dead, but flew away with my arrow in it. No one seemed very thrilled by my story, and later I found the arrow suspiciously near the spot from which I'd fired it.

We made splendid tree houses, using nothing that Swiss Family Robinson would not have had with them on the island, and spent hours sitting in them talking, while Pud, my pony and Tommy, Nu's donkey, happily ate bits of hazel leaves and twigs below.

My pony, Pud, a strawberry roan with a snow white rump, with large chestnut spots on the white, was very fat and made a particularly satisfactory zebra; but Nu had less success with Tommy, who looked less like the ostrich he was supposed to be, and who objected violently to having hen feathers tied to his head and tail.

Saddles—or the lack of them—were no problem anyway, as we always road bareback. Mamma said that she didn't mind if we fell off and were killed cleanly, but she didn't want us to be dragged for miles with our foot in a stirrup, as a cousin of ours had been not long before we were born. Riding Pud and Tommy, though, without bridles, using only strings of ivy to guide them, wasn't so good. They both knew their way home of course, and went there immediately and without fuss. The ivy halters didn't bother them at all.

CHAPTER II

Grandma must have had a special Guardian Angel when dealing with us; I remember one awful evening, the gong had gone for tea, which we always had in the breakfast room on the ground floor. On this terrible day, Nu laid herself along the second step from the top of the stairs. When Grandma came out of the drawing room, I called from the bottom of the stairs: "Can you see Nu, Grandma? She's quite near you." Grandma looked round, and then to our horror, she merely said "No," and began coming down the stairs. Naturally her foot landed at once on Nu's back, and trying not to tread on her too heavily, Grandma fell to the bottom of the stairs. We were terrified; it was a flight of twelve steps, and Grandma bumped down all of them and on to the marble floor of the hall.

14

Marian, the parlourmaid, hearing our screams and the noise of the fall, rushed out of the pantry, all 18 stone of her, crossing herself and crying out "God help us, herself is gone." But she took charge and lifted Grandma up, who to our tearful relief, wasn't gone but was very shaken.

How we hadn't killed her, I cannot think; but at the time Nu and I were quite certain she was dead, and never before had we known such utter misery, as we stared at her—lying still and silent—a black heap on the floor. We talked it over endlessly afterwards, and decided that had Grandma died, we would have run away and worked for the rest of our lives in the middle of a town. This the most horrifying punishment we could devise for ourselves.

I don't think that Grandma ever told Marian what had made her fall. I think she knew that we would never have been forgiven for our wickedness—Marian had a really violent temper.

Nu and I lived at Coole for the whole of our early life, and while my brother Richard had to go to boarding school in England at a very early age, we were able to stay on, being taught by a series of useless governesses and finally by Grandma herself.

Our governesses didn't mean much in our lives. I suppose they may have taught us something, but I can't remember actually doing lessons with any of them.

Two of them I can remember. One, Miss Roberts, was famous because she ran over me in the pony trap.

It was all very dramatic. Coming to the Lodge gate one day, we found that Laurence wasn't there to open it. I hopped out, and before the gate was fully open Miss Roberts let Pud go. He dashed for home, knocking me over, and the wheels of the trap went over my legs. It really was very painful, but Miss Roberts went next day, so it was well worth it.

We also had a young—I suppose she was young, I remember she had a very pink and white face, and damp podgy hands—French Governess, 'Mamzelle'. I have no idea of her name, I doubt if anyone

15

had, and she didn't stay very long. I don't remember speaking a single word of French, but I had seen her rushing—stark naked—down the long passage at the back of the house, and merely thought that this was a French habit. I was thrilled to be able to tell Nu what a *very* strange shape French people were. All large and wobbly. I was *sure* that Irish people didn't look like that with no clothes on. Very soon after this we were told that Mamzelle had been taken ill and had had to go home. I asked if she'd caught cold from running about with no clothes on, but with a horrified look, I was told: "Oh no child, don't be disgusting. She went mad."

Grandma taught us to read and write—and also arithmetic and French. Grandma wasn't very good at arithmetic, so when we finally went to school, we were put in the lowest form for maths; but we used to get very good marks in English and Scripture.

Our French was quite good too—except for our accent. We had a very tough French Mistress at school. Wire-thin, wearing a bun and pince-nez. She was known as Fido, and spat all the time. Froth leapt from her mouth when she got angry. She frothed incessantly whenever Nu or myself read aloud in French; it was obviously almost more than she could bear.

One of our worst stumbling blocks was the word 'bonne'. Quite a simple word, one would think, but Grandma always pronounced it 'bun' and bun it remained for Nu and me—however hard we tried to say it as Fido kept telling us it should be pronounced. Everyone else in the room seemed to think we were terribly brave, and that we were defying Fido—she thought so too—but we really could not remember to change the word in time.

School was particularly trying for Nu and myself. We had never been away from home, and had never lived with dozens of other people eating and sleeping and breathing all around us. We didn't enjoy much of our time there. Nu hated every minute and I hated every minute except games. We seemed to go to chapel or church dozens of times a week. In church Nu was better off than I was, because she discovered that if she fainted, she was taken out at once, and allowed to rest for about an hour. She had never fainted in her life before but she developed an enormously convincing and breathy collapse. I was very jealous, but never had the nerve to try it out myself.

Till we went to school, the only time we'd left home was to go to London for about six months during the bad times.

Mamma had been the sole survivor of an ambush. It was all rather horrible and nightmarish. Grandma had gone to stay with Bernard Shaw, and Mamma had gone to a tennis party one Sunday, early after lunch. She had been picked up by a party from the barracks at Gort. I can remember quite clearly them going off, because we had met them all except one very young officer. I remember Mrs Blake very clearly; Nu and I used to copy her deep voice, in some of our games.

I naturally don't remember how we spent the afternoon, but when we were having our supper in the tiny dining-room that evening, John Diveney came up the stone staircase from the kitchen; we heard his boots clanking on the stone floor, and then heard him saying in a hoarse whisper to Marian, "We must fetch her Ladyship home. It's terrible." And then something in a lower whisper which we couldn't hear. "God save us," we heard Marian gasp, "Isn't that a fright?" More whispering from John, and then Marian's footsteps hurrying up to the nursery to tell Ellen.

We were wild with expectation and full of self-made rumours. I know I was certain that Sukie had had a calf with two heads, having read that a local circus had a two-headed one on show—and Nu was equally convinced that the apple garden had been raided and that John had caught one of the raiders.

Neither of us for a moment thought that Mamma might possibly have been involved in anything. She was far too exhalted a person to be in an accident or anything like that.

Next morning we asked Ellen after breakfast what all the excite-

17

ment had been about, and she said that the people Mamma had been with had had an accident *but that* Mamma was all right, and not hurt at all.

John Diveney went to fetch her in the side car, and we ran alongside him down the avenue asking him what sort of an accident had Mamma been in. "Ahh, 'twas no accident Miss Anne," he said " 'twas no accident at all."

This was more intriguing than anything we had thought of on our own, and we dashed back to Ellen, pestering her to tell us what had really happened. Finally she told us that the car that Mamma was in had been attacked by blackguards, and that everyone had been shot dead except Mamma; she was quite all right, but had spent the night with the Bagots, where the car had been ambushed at the gates.

I remember quite vividly my immediate reaction: "Oh, I *am* glad that they were in a Ford and not in the side car, or Cobje might have been shot."

The aftermath of this was about the grimmest time I can remember at Coole.

Mamma was very shaken, and either Nu or I had to sleep with her in her enormous four poster bed every night. *How* we hated it. It was all so embarrassing—the nearness of this astral being—clad in a nightdress, and—oh horrors—snoring.

After about a week Mamma couldn't stand it any longer either, and to our enormous relief, she said she would be all right without us, as Grandma was coming home.

It wasn't very long after this that Nu and I were in the Nut Wood—we were stalking a rabbit actually—when suddenly we came on two men hiding in a small clearing who leapt round and pointed rifles at us when they heard us. They apparently knew at once who we were, though we didn't recognise them, and they insisted on walking back with us along the path right up to the big double wooden gates into the flower garden. They were terribly nice, and didn't look very old, and told us that they were living in the woods at the moment, but that whatever we did we must not come into the woods at all for at least three days—because there were a lot of men in it on the run, and we might get hurt by mistake.

We told Grandma, and she explained that though they carried rifles, and alas, sometimes used them, they were really kind decent men who wouldn't let little girls get hurt.

We told her that one of the men had said, "Tell Her Ladyship that we wouldn't hurt a hair of anyone in Her Ladyship's family," and we were rather horrified because we thought she was crying, but she said she had a cold coming and it always made her nose and eyes run very fast, so we were quite happy about the whole thing.

CHAPTER III

It was after this that we had to leave Coole for England for the first time. Mamma was terrified that we would get shot, so she took us back to London with her when she went.

It was the first time that Nu and I had been out of Ireland, and though we hated leaving Coole, we were rather thrilled at the thought of travelling across Ireland in a train, and the idea of crossing the whole way to England in a boat was very exciting. We had never been in anything bigger than a rowing boat—either on the lake at Coole, or at Burren, and we couldn't think how we were all going to fit in a boat with the masses of luggage we had with us.

It was a long journey in the train, but there were lots of things to look at, and we had a wonderful hamper of food. Grandma came with us as far as the Broadstone, as she was going to the Abbey anyway, she said, and then we went on alone with Mamma to the boat.

When we got to the quay everything was rather frightening, with people hurrying about, and porters all carrying masses of cases, and there seemed to be bells ringing everywhere. Mamma got a porter to take all our luggage, and we got out of the train, clinging to our 'nose-bags' that Grandma had given us. Grandma always gave everybody a nose-bag when they went on a journey—a paper bag with sweets, buns and an apple in it.

We looked round us as we hurried. It was dark except for the lights all along the platform, and we couldn't see either the sea or a boat. Mamma told us to keep close—she needn't have, we were terrified we'd get lost—and she walked up a sort of bridge sloping up at an awful angle. I was terrified; I peered for a minute over the side and thought I saw water below. When we stepped off the narrow bridge, we were on some sort of planks, and then we went through a door, over a very high narrow step, into a very large room. There was an extraordinary smell. It was a sort of mixture of oil and heat and metal, and not at all nice, and like nothing we had ever smelt before. "Hope it smells better when we get on the boat," I said to Nu, "I don't like this at all." "I'll be sick if I stay here for long." Nu said in a determined voice.

We then went down some super stairs, far wider than the stairs at Coole, into an enormous room, with chairs and tables in the middle, and beds all round the sides, one bed above another, and with real curtains to pull across them.

"Wherever are we?" I asked Mamma, in surprise, "when do we get on the boat?"

"This *is* the boat," said Mamma, "and here are your bunks," and she walked over to the side of the room.

"This isn't a *boat*," I wailed, "This isn't a boat, this is just a drawing-room." We were miserable about it. It was no more a boat than the drawing-room at Coole, except that of course there were no bunks in the Coole drawing room.

We undressed and got into our two bunks, as Mamma told us to, and she went off to have a meal before she went to bed.

There was an awful lot of ringing of bells, and we could hear men shouting outside, and then the men's voices stopped, and the creaking began. The boat began shuddering and shaking, and then literally seemed to go on its side, and the noise of things falling about was terrific.

Nu and I were very frightened, but almost worse, we began to feel terribly sick. All the women in bunks round us seemed to be being sick, and both of us began to look round for something to be sick into. We had just located a sort of tin charlie, when Mamma came back into the room. Seeing what we were doing, she seized the charlies out of our hands, and in a furious voice she said: "You are not to be sick. No Gregory was ever sick. I have never been sick, and you are not to be. Don't be so common!" We were so frightened of Mamma when she was cross, that we swallowed manfully, and we weren't sick—though the lady in the white uniform who seemed to be in charge, said to us that we were the only people in the room except herself that hadn't been ill, and she thought we were marvellous. So Nu and I felt a little less miserable, and managed to behave ourselves all right until we got to London, where we were to stay for about six months.

I have never in all my life been so desperately unhappy. Mamma had a very large house right on the river at Hammersmith Mall, with what I suppose was a large garden. The whole thing to us was absolute misery, and our only moment of real deep happiness was reading the typed weekly letter from Grandma telling us everything about Coole and about all our things there, and whenever she sent great parcels of moss and little red toadstools on twigs from the Nut Wood, we made great flat dishes of them, and sniffed and sniffed the lovely wet mossy smell and imagined that we were back at our beloved Coole.

I think it was because we were such a miserable and unattractive

22

couple that we were allowed to go home sooner than had been arranged.

Mamma couldn't take us back when the time came, so she hired a 'Universal Aunt' to travel with us to Coole. This 'Universal Aunt' was a very tall thin woman, with a long pink nose, and obviously disliked children. Not that we minded in the least what she was like, we were so deliriously happy at going home.

I don't remember much of the journey, though I do seem to remember that we were rather embarrassed a couple of times by the Universal Aunt making very odd remarks to porters, but when we got on the boat, we began telling her about Mamma's ambush. She re-acted so splendidly and in such a terrified manner, that Nu and I invented a great number of other stories of shootings and killings at Coole and in the woods around. By the time we docked, the Aunt was virtually hysterical. She took us to the Standard Hotel, and left us! As she went out of the door, she shouted: "I'm not going to stay here and be shot by murderers, you can look after yourselves from now on."

We were quite amazed by all this, but luckily the staff at the 'Standard' knew Grandma well, as she always stayed there, and though we had to spend a night there on our own until Grandma managed to get a train up from Coole, we were quite all right. I remember that it was the first telegram I had ever sent on my own. Nu and I had a very interesting time composing it. I think we said: "Lady Gregory Coole Park Gort Co. Galway Ireland"—then remembered that as we were *in* Ireland, we could leave that out. We started the message: "Universal Aunt" then we weren't sure whether it really *was* universal, and anyway weren't sure of the spelling, so we continued "Aunt ..." realised that this seemed very odd, as Aunt Ruth and Aunt Gladys weren't there and Grandma might be annoyed thinking it was one of them who'd left us stranded, so we decided to say: "Lady hired by Mamma to bring us to Coole has gone back to London and left us at the Standard Hotel, Harcourt Street, Dublin. We have no money, what shall we do? Tons of love Anne and Catherine." Nu wouldn't let me put Nu on the telegram: she said that the Post Office might laugh.

Nu wasn't her real name, it was actually a name she'd given herself when she was very young. People said to her "you do that" and she'd answer: "yes Nu do that" as she did it, so she became Nu.

Whether the lady in the desk at the hotel sent our telegram as we wrote it, I don't know, but we got a wire saying "Arriving tomorrow to bring you home. Love Grandmamma." and I must say we were very relieved to get it, as we had been discussing what we could do if Grandma didn't get our wire, and we were left for ever at the Standard.

Grandma arrived next day in time for tea. It was so lovely to see her, and we were deliriously happy as we sat down together to an enormous spread.

It was the first time that we had had a meal with Grandma in a hotel.

It was so awful. When we'd finished tea, Grandma took a used envelope out of her purse, and tipped all the sugar left in the sugar basin into it, folded it up, and put it back in her purse. Nu and I went scarlet with embarrassment. Grandma *stealing*? We were in agonies lest the waitress would notice that there wasn't a single lump left, and ask what we'd done with it. I think this was the only thing that Grandma ever did to upset us at all. She always did the same thing, and I tried to pretend that I wanted to go to the lav. just before the end of every meal, so as not to see her doing it. Nu once asked her why she took all the sugar, and Grandma said that as she had paid for it and never took sugar in her tea, she didn't see why she should leave it for them to sell to someone else.

CHAPTER IV

It must have been some time before this that Bernard Shaw was staying with us. He came quite a lot when we were very small, but later on he hardly came at all. He seemed enormously tall to Nu and me, and we often wondered if he had to brush and comb his beard, like our hair, every day. We didn't dare to ask him outright, and though we hinted quite a lot, he didn't answer.

While there were visitors at Coole, Grandma didn't read to us, but we always went to the library or drawing room for about an hour after tea, before going on up to bed.

G.B.S. was one of the nicest visitors at Coole, and always said that he'd play a game with us. I can't really remember playing any game with him, except 'Hunt the Thimble.' He was very good at this game, and was incredibly quick at spotting where we'd hidden the thimble which infuriated Nu and me, as we could usually fox other adults, and even each other, sometimes. I'm not quite sure when or how it dawned on us, that G.B.S. was *cheating*. It started as a sort of awkward feeling that he went too directly to the place we'd hidden the thimble; he couldn't *always* be so clever? . . . and then one evening—having talked it over earlier in the day—we arranged that I would watch him through my fingers while Nu hid the thimble. (I gave Nu my solemn word that I wouldn't look at *her* at all.) To my utter horror I saw G.B.S. turn round—quite blatantly—and *look* . . . definitely look through his fingers where Nu was hiding it.

It was so *embarrassing*. A grown-up actually cheating. I had never been in a situation like this before. You couldn't accuse a grown-up of cheating, but you couldn't possibly play 'Hunt the Thimble' when you were bound to lose every time. The whole thing was unthinkable—and I did the only thing I could think of on the spur of the moment—I burst into a flood of tears. I did this fairly easily—either involuntarily or on purpose—and had found that one didn't have to explain the reason for the flood, until the noise and dampness had gone.

G.B.S. was very upset, and kept on pressing me to tell him what was wrong, and he was sure that he could make it better. But how could I tell him that I was howling because he'd been cheating for days and days. I was sent up to bed in disgrace, Nu with me, which was bad luck for her, but when she heard about G.B.S. she was as shattered as I was by the horror of the whole thing. Luckily G.B.S. was leaving the next day, so we were spared the awfulness of having to decide what to do about playing with him again.

In the evening we told Grandma about it, and how awful it all was. Grandma laughed till the tears fell down on to her lap.

G.B.S. wasn't *cheating*! he thought we'd seen him looking all the time and thought it was a joke, and that he was making the game more amusing. We were far from amused, secretly feeling that it might seem funny to a grown-up, but to us it was still dishonest; though we felt rather bad that we had actually accused him of such a big crime, if he really didn't think it was such a terrible thing to do.

However, at Grandma's suggestion later we collected a lot of his favourite apples—croftons that grew on two terrifically old trees in the apple garden, and Grandma packed them up, and posted them to him 'with love from Anne and Catherine to G.B.S.' Grandma wanted us to put 'with love from Anne and Catherine to their kind playmate G.B.S.' but we definitely couldn't bring ourselves to do this.

Some weeks after sending the apples, we got an envelope addressed to 'The Misses Catherine and Anna Gregory' and inside was a poem from G.B.S. written by him on the back of five picture postcards, thanking us for the apples.

> Two ladies of Galway, called Catherine and Anna,
> Whom some call Acushla and some call Alanna
> On finding the gate of the fruit garden undone
> Stole Grandmamma's apples and sent them to London.
>
> And Grandmamma said that the poor village schoolchildren
> Were better behaved than the well-brought-up Coole children
> And threatened them with the most merciless whippings
> If ever again they laid hands on her pippins.
>
> In vain they explained that the man who was battening
> On Grandmamma's apples would die without fattening
> > She seized the piano
> > And threw it at Anna
> Then shrieking at Catherine "Just let me catch you"
> She walloped her hard with the drawing-room statue.
> "God save us, Herself is gone crazy" cried Marian
> "Is this how a lady of title should carry on?"
> "If you dare to address me like that," shouted Granny,
> "Goodbye to your wages: you shan't have a penny:
> Go back to your pots and your pans and your canisters"
> With that she threw Marian over the banisters.

"And now" declared Granny, "I feel so much better
That I'll write Mr Shaw a most beautiful letter
And tell him how happy our lives are at Coole
Under Grandmamma Darling's beneficent rule."

It took a little time for me to really enjoy the poem, because it began
Catherine and Anna, instead of Anne and Catherine, and anyway my
name was Anne and not Anna.

Grandma explained carefully that very often things had to be altered to
fit a poem, and that this didn't mean that he thought I was the younger by
putting me last, or by getting my name wrong.

Some time after this W. B. Yeats wrote a poem for me alone, and again
wasn't entirely pleased to start with. I felt it was very doggerelly and not
as romantic as I would have liked.

Mr Yeats sent a message for me to go up to his sitting-room, and then
said that he had written a poem called 'Yellow Hair' and that he had
dedicated it to me, and proceeded to read it, in his 'humming' voice. We
used to hear his voice 'humming' away for hours while he wrote his verse.
He used to hum the rhythm of a verse before he wrote the words,
Grandma told us, and that was why his poems are so good to read aloud.
That is what Grandma said, but on this occasion I was petrified. I had no
idea that he was going to write a poem to me, and had no idea at all what
one should say when he had read it aloud.

It was agony! For once, I think I did the right thing. Nearly in tears
for fear of doing something silly, "Read it again," I pleaded, "oh do
read it to me again."

Obviously this was all right, for Yeats beamed, put on his pince nez
attached to the broad black silk ribbon, and read it through again.

> Never shall a young man,
> Thrown into despair
> By those great honey-coloured
> Ramparts at your ear,
> Love you for yourself alone
> And not your yellow hair.

29

But I can get a hair-dye
And set such colour there,
Brown or black or carrot,
That young men in despair
Shall love me for myself alone
And not my yellow hair.

I heard an old religious man
But yesternight declare
That he had found a text to prove
That only God, my dear,
Could love you for yourself alone
And not your yellow hair.

This time I was able to stutter: "Wonderful. Thank you so much. Wonderful. I must go and wash my hair," and crashed out.

Years later Yeats broadcast some of his works on one of the first radio programmes from Belfast. He announced the next poem, saying it was dedicated to the granddaughter of his old friend Lady Gregory and that she had "hair like a cornfield in the sun." This time I was thrilled, and 'Yellow Hair' sounded really rather splendid. I had a couple of boy friends staying and they were very impressed too.

Next morning there was an envelope by my plate, in it was a poem 'To Anne G. . . . after WBY."

I was thrilled. Boy friend coming up to scratch at last, I thought. What Bliss! I opened the envelope, took out the poem and read:

If I was alone on an island,
And only Anne with me there,
I'd make myself cushions and bolsters,
By stuffing her skin with her hair.

CHAPTER V

Mr Yeats used to stay with us at Coole from as far back as I can remember.

There was a large bed of sedum in the flower garden, by the first vinery; in the summer it was alive with butterflies and I can remember Mamma once saying that sedum flowered all through the summer; and while it was in flower Yeats would be at Coole.

He always seemed to be there, leaning back in his chair at table—huge, with (in our eyes) an enormous tummy. He wore a signet ring with an enormous stone in it on his little finger, and Nu and I used to giggle like mad, and say he expected everyone to kiss it, like the Pope. She and I used to copy his habit of running his fingers through the great lock of hair that fell forward over his forehead, and then hold out our hand with the imaginary ring, saying: "This ring is a holy ring; it has been in touch with my holy halo."

We all lunched and had tea together. Nu and I didn't dine with the grown-ups, but Richard sometimes did.

Marian always waited at table at dinner, and Richard told us that Mr Yeats always sat with his chair pushed back much farther from the table than anyone else, and every time Marian passed behind him, she used to kick the back leg of his chair, by accident on purpose, and then say, "I'm sorry Sir, I never saw you had pulled back from the table." Richard said Marian did it over and over again, and Mr Yeats never moved his chair in by one inch. Nu and I dared each other to kick his chair leg at tea, but we never dared.

Mr Yeats didn't speak much—while we were there anyway—and seemed sunk in thought, miles away, though he never seemed to miss any food. Grandma always seemed to be filling his cup, which he passed up the moment it was empty, without looking up and without a word.

"Manners" Nu and I used to signal to each other with a disapproving look: "did you see? No please or thank you."

We had tea outside the front door on the gravel sweep every day in the summer and it never rained.

Mr Yeats sat on the garden chair that had wooden arms and a high back. Grandma sat on the green painted garden seat with curled iron arms and a back that curved over backwards, and we children had wicker stools with four legs, made by the travelling basket maker. They were made from withies and dogwood that grew on the side of the avenue Yellow willow and red dogwood, and they had very comfortable slightly concave circular seats, and were just the right height for the tables. The tables were really just pieces of polished mahogany that folded in half Marian and Ellen used to carry them out and put them on low trestles

32

and then Marian carried the enormous silver tray with the silver teapot with the acorn on the lid, and the enormous silver hot water jug, and then all the food. Masses of scones and butter and honey and strawberry jam bottled by Grandma, and lots of sponge cakes that Mary made, and which never tasted so heavenly as in the sun.

Mr Yeats actually seemed to talk more when he had tea out of doors, though he still passed his cup without a word, and anyway we often had visitors for tea in the summer.

It was great fun when people came to tea, when we were having it out of doors, because they had to drive up to the front door, virtually up to the tea table. The horses or ponies were taken down to the yard to be looked after by John Diveney, but later there were motor cars, and they merely passed the house, and parked under the enormous Ilex just beyond.

The workmen's bell was fixed in this tree, and was rung at 8.0 a.m., 12.0 noon, 1.0 p.m. and 6.0 p.m. for the starting and stopping of work. It was a lovely bell but woe betide any of us if we rang it at any other hour; though sometimes if Grandma wanted someone from the yard or garden she would tell us to go and give the bell "two swings only," which was a thrill.

You could hear the bell nearly three miles away, and the 12 o'clock bellringing meant that however hard pressed Nu and I were, even if our camp was surrounded by Indians, we had to make a determined effort and break out within a few minutes or we'd be late for lunch.

This was one of the few unbreakable rules. We had to be back in the house in time to wash our hands and get tidy before the gong went for lunch, and I cannot remember that we were ever late.

When the Indians were becoming less dangerous—I think we had driven them off so often that they were less anxious to attack—we began to turn our minds to decorating and beautiful houses.

Near the house, on the way down to the flower garden, there was a wonderful place where old laurels had grown into an archway, making a

33

natural entrance to a cave of dark green inside. The removal of a lot of dead wood was fairly easy, and the result was fantastic. A room big enough to carry in a bench and an enormous case that we found in the Haggart. It was easy to find an old table cloth, and we managed to slip out a bedspread for the 'sofa,' and we spent several admiring hours here.

However, to have a beautiful interior is not enough. It's all right if the outside has to be disguised to prevent the enemy locating you, but *this* house was for show. It was on the edge of the direct route Grandma or any visitor took from the house to the flower garden, and therefore it must look beautiful and intriguing from the path.

I had a passion for laburnum. I could think of nothing more beautiful than waking in the morning with laburnum growing across my bedroom window in great masses, with the sun shining golden through the flowers on to my bed. So here was my first real chance. I picked a lot of large branches of laburnum covered in tight buds, and planted them either side of the entrance to our mansion.

Then we decided that a mansion must have an avenue—with daffodils. The daffs were out, so we dug up a great number in the woods and planted an avenue of them up to the front door. The ground was very hard and we had great difficulty in making the holes deep enough to cover the bulbs, but we propped the flowers up with sticks, certain that in the morning they would have righted themselves and be standing high and firm. This was perhaps one of the worst disappointments we had known.

It was such a wonderful thing we had planned—the whole rather dark place, glowing with yellow daffodils followed by hanging lanterns of golden laburnum.

Next morning we rushed down to see our lovely house. It was shocking. We could see at once that the laburnum had wilted and was collapsed on the floor—lifeless. That was bad enough, but where were the daffodils? Had they been eaten or what? They'd vanished.

Very slowly we approached, wondering if some horrible animal would rise from the ground, perhaps still chewing the final flower.

And then we saw a few pathetic yellow forms lying on the ground, their colour nearly gone, and looking so tiny and so *few*. Surely we'd planted ten times that number?

It was awful!

It was awful that it *looked* so awful, and it was awful that we had moved the daffs and they were dead, and we had killed them, and it was awful that now no-one would come and admire our new house. I don't think that I have ever been so completely miserable.

Sean O'Casey was staying with us at this time, and he wandered past, gazing at the trees as he seemed to do a great deal of the time. He didn't know the names of the different trees and Grandma was teaching him. He had funny pink eyes and he saw us—or even probably heard us sobbing.

"What's up with you," he asked us kindly enough, "have you hurt yourselves?"

"No," we tried to be grown-up. "No, we've had trouble with our avenue. The daffodils don't like being divided like this. They were all together, and we think they're *lonely*." This was invented on the spur of the moment, but we suddenly thought it might be true.

"Ah well," said Mr O'Casey, "don't waste your time on lonely daffodils, there's plenty more would welcome your tears."

We were sure he said this. It sounded very silly to us. Who would want our tears more than our poor dead daffs, killed by our own hands. Before we got too soaked with tears Grandma came along with our elevenses. Dear, dear, Grandma. One glance at the shambles.

"Goodness," she said, "what a wonderful idea making an avenue like that. It will be *so* beautiful next year—like a fairy road and if you are at school I'll see them coming up and I'll be able to write to you both and tell you about them, and it will make me think of you both every time I go to the flower garden."

"But Grandma," we wailed, "they're dead. We've killed them."

"Nonsense," said Grandma, "they're not *dead*. They may be sulking because they were having a party when you dug them up; but next year they will come up again as bright as buttons. You can never really dig up a flower when it is open and cheerful and obviously having a good time. It resents it. But when it's faded you can, because then it rather likes the idea of going somewhere new," and Grandma came into our house with our elevenses and sat on the sofa and didn't ask where we'd got the bedspread from.

CHAPTER VI

The lake at Coole was a wonderful place, though Nu and I really preferred the woods, especially the Nut Wood which was the most friendly. Masses of deep thick moss and nut bushes and big trees and pigeons, and the paths a mass of violets and primroses. However, the water for the house was pumped up from the lake every day.

There was a large pump near the lake. The pump was a long way from the water's edge in the summer, but in the winter the water rose and sometimes it got covered by the floods and it was very difficult to get to it then.

Every day Charlie, the very tall bay horse with a white face, was harnessed to the long spar, and walked round and round pumping the water up from the lake, through the pipes across the hobble field and the corner of the back lawn and up the top of the house.

Fascinating things used to appear in our bath water. Small snails, moss, leaves and once there was a tiny animal that we were sure was a baby trout. Though once Mamma found a leech in her bath, and we heard her telling Grandma about this with horror, and saying that it might have stuck to her and drained her of all her blood.

After this we didn't really like our bath quite so much, and were terrified of being sucked dry—though Ellen always said that "herself was always imagining things, and sure there were none of them animals in Coole at all."

Nu and I used to go and drive Charlie round and round sometimes, though only if we had happened to go that way *en route* to somewhere. It wasn't very exciting after a few minutes, as one couldn't see anything happening—no rushing of water past as it went to the house; though there was a small hole near the pump which was supposed to fill with water when the tanks were full.

I don't think that it ever worked properly though, because Mary the cook nearly always had to rush out and pull the workmen's bell three times to tell Mike that the tank was overflowing. Mike used to sit on the shaft sucking his old pipe and gazing into the distance, and I don't think he ever looked at the hole to see if it was full anyway.

Much more exciting than driving Charlie round and round the pump at Coole, was driving the horses round and round threshing down in Burren. This was *thrilling*. There were two horses to be driven—one on either end of the pole, and there was a terrible revolving bar which one had to step over on every circuit. The horses seemed very clever at stepping over this bar, but I was never without a secret fear that I would trip and fall and be run over by the other horse coming behind me. The horses had to be kept going at a steady pace—not too slowly or the grain didn't separate properly—not too fast or the whole machine might collapse. It was a tremendous responsibility, and we took it with great seriousness.

While we walked round and round, the whole field seemed solid with noise, straw and dust. The throbbing roar and shake of the great machine. Men shouting as they threw the sheaves up on forks to others above, who caught them deftly, untied them, and spread them flat, riffling them into the jaws of the thresher, to be shaken and torn apart, the corn arriving at the other end, filling sack after sack; while the straw—now beheaded—was endlessly removed from under the machine by more men with pitchforks.

Straw, chaff and dust seemed to be everywhere—in our hair and in our clothes and sticking to our bare legs. We got hotter and hotter as we shouted "Go on outa that. Hup—hup" to our respective horses. And every now and again a great roar of encouragement from Pat Tierney "Dat's right Miss Anne, keep him going sthrong. Ye're a great girl, God bless you," and a renewed yell of "Hup, Hup" from me, feeling my face get hotter and hotter with praise and the responsibility.

When the time came for a pause for rest and refreshment, Pat came down from feeding the thresher, and took up the rein of my horse saying that the horse always knew from his voice the way to stop going, he would give a terrific roar of "Whoa, whoa now let yez Whoa" and both horses took two or three steps and stopped as one. Incredible the silence after the roar and clanking of machinery and the shouts of the men, and our own yells of encouragement to the horses.

Everyone had cups of tea or bottles of porter; but Nu and I always ran home while they were resting. People seemed to be rather silly, and seemed to be tickling each other and screaming with laughter, and Pat's sisters who were nice friendly shy girls seemed to go quite mad, screaming louder than the rest, and we felt faintly out of place and suddenly unwanted. The work was one thing—we were part of that—and everyone

39

said what a great help we were, but afterwards it was so different and we hurried away before we felt embarrassed.

Later on, when we heard the shouts of men's voices and the machine working, we'd go back and at once were caught up in the thrill of the whole thing once again.

At the end of the day, Pat Tierney's father, called 'Old Sugar' said he must pay us a man's wage for a man's work, but we were very embarrassed by this, and said that we must go home, but may we come again tomorrow please. Old Sugar said weren't we the great girls to be after doing such a great day's work, and we felt well paid. Why we called Mr Tierney 'Old Sugar' I can't remember.

We never went to anyone else's thrashing, it wasn't the same at all, and no one else seemed to want two experienced drivers, they never asked us, but the Tierneys always asked if we'd be free on such and such a date, as they needed us to help them.

CHAPTER VII

Burren was heaven. The house itself—Mount Vernon—was lovely, with lovely bare floors that didn't mind sand or seaweed on them, and bright pots on the mantelpieces.

The mantelpieces were very exciting, made of brick—all little shelves and overhanging pieces, and decorated with coloured tiles with strange animals painted on them. Mamma said that she and Dada had designed the mantelpieces with Augustus John, and that they had built them themselves, and that Dada and Augustus John had had awful fights about the best way to lay the bricks. We used to examine the mantelpiece in our playroom, and seeing the odd brick not quite straight, used—with great

41

loyalty—to say "there is a brick that Augustus John laid, Dada wouldn't have put one in crooked like that."

Spring tides were one of our high spots. We used to go down on the sand with buckets and spades to dig up sea urchins or razor fish. We soon learned that a small open hole was the breathing hole for a razor fish, and we crept to it to begin digging, because if we stamped overhead the razor fish would hear us and begin digging even before we did. They travelled so fast anyway, that we very seldom managed to dig one out though sometimes we did feel our spade grate on the shell and we yelled with excitement or encouragement—but he still burrowed more quickly than we could dig.

'Lord Grip'—whose real name was Mr Minogue—was always on the shore at Spring Tide, and he had no difficulty in filling his bucket with razor fish. We were rather frightened of him. We knew he'd been christened Lord Grip by Mamma because he nipped everything, and we kept looking round to see that our shrimping net and home-made harpoon were still where we'd left them. His daughter 'The Honourable' Hetty, used to work at spring tides, her skirts tucked up above her knees as she walked backwards and forwards up to her waist in water, pulling carrageen moss from the rocks. This she laid out on the grass beside the road to dry, and we knew that at night the amount of her carrageen more than doubled as she took the moss collected by other women and laid out along the Flaggy Shore to put with her own.

The Honourable Hetty used to come along to Mount Vernon with various things to sell, and we were thrilled but rather scared the wonderful time when Mamma bought three chickens from her. . . . "sure they're the fattest hins in Burren, and why wouldn't they be, the oats and potatoes I've been putting into them all the winter so that yer honour could have the fine birds for the childer." It was unfortunate that our only other neighbour in Burren should have come in a few hours later complaining about her three hens that had been stolen overnight, and

42

walked straight into the yard where Katie was picking them. I don't think she ever really believed that *we* hadn't taken them.

Lord Grip and his son used to belt at full gallop along the road between the sea and field in front of the house, going off up the hills to look for a strayed bullock, or to search along the Flaggy Shore for driftwood. Lord Grip rode an old black horse, its hip bones standing out stark even at distance, and his son Mike rode a jennet. We always stood to watch them as they rode bareback past with shouts and such a clatter of hoofs. We always wondered whether it was their bullocks they were going to round up, or if they were off on some other plot.

Shrimping was much more rewarding than digging for the razor fish and we caught masses of shrimps, but it never really seemed worth while shelling the tiny things, so unless we caught big ones, or prawns, we didn't bother to bring them home, after the first meal off them. There were also an enormous number of small green crabs, which we couldn't believe wouldn't be delicious to eat. However, Katie insisted that they were poison, and so we used to put a lot of these in the pond at the bottom of the field in front of the house, which was full of rocks and filled with water at spring tides, the sea coming into it under the road. Sometimes if it was a very high spring tide the whole of the bottom of the field was covered with sea water, and when it receded the grass all around was covered with the shells of long dead crabs.

Old Francie, the postman, was the only person in the district who had a boat, or who would dare to go out on the sea at all. None of the people living at Burren had ever been out in a boat, not even to try to catch a mackerel; and on Fridays, when a car came round from Galway with fish in it, they would flock to buy the limp white bits of fish that had travelled about 20 miles by road.

There were a lot of mackerel in the bay, and we caught a lot. I never liked the bait Francie used—a small bit of skin from an old dog fish or something equally evil for the first bait, but after that a slip cut from the side of the first mackerel we caught, cut from it the moment it came into

43

the boat. I hated this. However, there came a time when Grandma gave us each a special bait, a tiny spinning spoon with a hook with three prongs on it.

Such a wonderful invention. Only Grandma could have found such a thing. Francie was suitably impressed. "The mackerel will fall over themselves to get at them things," he said, "and why wouldn't they?" I don't remember that the mackerel did fall over themselves to get at the spinners, and Francie still caught more fish than we did with his bits of fish. Horrible cannibals.

One of the most exciting things about Burren was the number of thrilling things that got washed up on the shore after a storm.

Turf was brought to the quay at Burren in pookhawns; it was stacked in the holds piled high above the decks, and a lot got swept off when there was rough weather.

We had a go-cart, with a seat at either end, that we were now far too big to be pushed in, and this was a wonderful carrier for all the things we picked up along the Flaggy Shore.

Sometimes we'd fill the go-cart easily with great sods of turf, and come home with enough to keep the kitchen range going for a whole day. At other times we'd only find two or three good pieces, half hidden under streams of seaweed; but we might find a lot of wood, which was nearly as good, and which we burned on the play-room fire, and which always burned with such a strange blue flame. The grown-ups said that this was the salt in the wood, which we thought was a bit silly. It was obviously foreign wood, and foreign wood was bound to burn differently from Irish wood.

All sorts of strange things were washed up. We found a baby's cot once. A great thrill. We had never had such a wonderful find before. It would make a wonderful bed for our dolls and animals—though we weren't really great doll lovers. But it was really big enough for us to climb into if we were very careful—and *fancy* finding such a thing on the *Flaggy shore*. It had remains of lace on it, very smart, and it must have come from America—straight across the Atlantic. We were thrilled and made up chilling stories of the cot floating out to sea with the baby in it. The baby had obviously been rescued as there was no skeleton in it, but in our heartless way, we didn't really feel much upset in any case.

We thought the grown-ups were being pretty stupid when they found us playing with the cot, and heard where we'd found it. "Little pagans" I heard Mamma say to Augustus John, who was staying at Coole and who had come down with her for the day, "I really can't let them grow up here like little savages. They will have go to school and get civilised and get some human feelings." Nu, who reported this conversation, said that John had answered something about ". . . innocence never really knowing grief, and leave them alone, they'll grow up to it only too quickly."

It all sounded rather silly, and I was certain that Nu had got the conversation all wrong, so sent her back to listen again; but she returned at once saying that they were now talking nonsense about someone called 'Mattress' a painter apparently who mixed up his colours. Grown ups!

CHAPTER VIII

Augustus John—when we were on our own we called him 'John,' copying
Mamma, who knew him very well—in fact she told us that he was Best
Man when she and Dada were married, which we thought was rather bad
luck on Dada—Augustus John used to stay at Coole a lot when we were

very young, but I don't remember much about him then. He was large and rather frightening to look at, and we felt he might step on us, as he seemed to stride about not ever looking where he was going.

He painted my brother, a very odd picture we thought, which was very like him in some ways, with his felt hat on the back of his head with the elastic under his chin, as he used to wear it when he was forced to wear a hat, but he had painted in enormous sticky-out ears and eyes that sloped up at the corners, rather like a picture of a chinaman we had seen in a book.

I know I was very pleased some years later when Mamma told me that John had wanted to paint *me* at the time, but that Grandma had insisted on the son of the house being painted and she was paying, but that Augustus John had been very annoyed at being thwarted, and had given Richard that funny look to pay Grandma out! The picture of Richard was hung in the drawing-room, on the left of the big fireplace.

The drawing-room was a lovely big room. It had an enormous big bay, the whole width of the room, with three separate great windows reaching from floor to ceiling. Grandma's desk was in the middle, out in front of the centre window, and in the window was a large white marble figure of Andromeda as large as life, sitting on a great marble rock. Sometimes if we lay on the floor in front of Grandma when she was writing, and got in exactly the right place, it looked as though Grandma had two heads—her own and a white marble one growing out of the top of hers, and it was great fun making the marble head come and disappear by moving ourselves up and down! Grandma had her typewriter on a very shaky table in the right hand window, and when Richard was away at school Grandma wrote to him on her typewriter, and Nu and I dictated in turn things that had happened to us or to Taddy or Pud or Tommy, and she added all this to her letter.

There was a simply enormous divan in the drawing-room, very low and covered with marvellous rugs and shawls, and with masses and masses of cushions piled up at the back. All over the wall above the cushions and the whole way along that wall, there were pictures of all sizes, in gilt frames, they really looked rather like a patch work quilt, there were so many different sizes and brilliant colours. I remember once, when we had been ragging on the divan, one of the brilliantly coloured rugs got pulled off on to the floor, and suddenly we saw that the marvellous divan was made of several layers of large mattresses— they looked slightly indecent, and Nu and I were very careful after that not to pull the rugs to show the rather shaming underneath.

There was an enormous chandelier in the middle of the room with about 50 candles in it. I only saw it lighted once or twice, as it was only lighted for parties. Marian had to get a step-ladder to light the candles, and after parties someone had to stand on a chair to snuff them out, even though there was a long snuffer for them.

I remember one awful story Mamma told us about the time they had a large party, and after dinner they played table-turning, and everyone got terrified, because of the messages that were coming on the table, so they put out the candles and went to bed. And next morning, Marian was absolutely furious, because when she came into the drawing-room, all the candles on the chandelier were all still alight. She stormed up to Dada's room, and told him that he might have burned the whole house down, that he had no right to go off to bed without blowing out the candles and she would never sleep peaceful again if the candles on the chandelier were left alight.

"But we put the candles out before we went to bed, Marian." Dada said, "I put them out myself."

"That you didn't, Master Robert," Marian snorted, "and you needn't think that I am climbing up to put them out neither!"

Dada couldn't think what she was talking about, and went down to the drawing-room to look, and sure enough—the candles were still burning, and the frightening thing was that they hadn't burnt down at all since the evening before and there was absolutely no grease dropping from them.

48

Nu and I were simply terrified of this story, and often looked nervously to see whether they had lighted up again.

I remember the thrill when Richard made his first wireless set.

It was the first wireless set that any one at Coole had seen—actually Nu and I hadn't an idea what a wireless set was meant to do, and when Richard brought it down to the drawing-room, and put it on the edge of the divan, and we heard the sounds of scratchy music coming through the headphones, we thought it was pure magic.

It was terribly clever of Richard to make this set. He built it all into the case that had had the musical box in it. I remember there were lots of valves and things, but the most impressive thing about it was the enormous accumulator which was attached to it. This sat on the floor by the set.

One day an awful thing happened. The accumulator leaked and the acid burned a large hole in the carpet. Mamma was furious as it was, apparently, a very valuable foreign carpet; but Grandma thought Richard was so clever to make the set work that she didn't mind the carpet: "You can't make omelettes without breaking eggs," she said. Nu and I looked with even greater awe at the set. Was Richard going to *cook* in it as well?

Grandma was absolutely thrilled with Richard's effort, and told him that he had a wonderful gift and that he might well be Ireland's greatest engineer of the century, but Nu and I still thought that it was a good deal to do with magic that made those sounds come through the headphones, and we kept an eye on the chandelier, to see if the candles did anything when the music was loudest.

In the corner of the drawing-room, on the left of the fireplace, there was another large marble statue of a lady standing up with no clothes on. She was Venus, and she was as large as Mamma. There was a sofa right across the front of Venus, and the space behind made a wonderful place to hide from grown-ups. Nu and I got hold of some of Mamma's cigarettes once, and retreated behind the sofa, and began smoking them. Grandma got very agitated about this, and told Mamma to tell us to come out and to stop smoking, but Mamma said "No, let them go on for as long as they can, they'll be terribly sick, and they'll never smoke again." So, pressed against the wall behind Venus's behind, Nu and I smoked about three cigarettes each, while Grandma watched us in horror, and Mamma in hopes, and when we finished all the cigarettes we had, we came out and we were never sick at all.

CHAPTER IX

All our lives Nu and I had a pony or a donkey to ride. Tommy was really Nu's donkey. He had started as Richard's but when Richard went to school he became Nu's.

Before he went to school there were two donkeys—Tommy and Sammy. Grandma had christened them because of the war or something. "A Tommy Atkins and Uncle Sam," she used to say, "they should be good friends." It didn't make any sense to us, but Tommy was much the nicest donkey. Sammy was nearly black, and much smaller, and Nu was a bit frightened of him, as he wasn't as good tempered as Tommy who was endlessly patient, and if he was particularly stubborn and refused to move at all, you could get off him, smack him heartily with a big stick, then climb up on him again while he remained rooted to the ground, and then with more yells and kicking heels and chucking of the reins, he might deign to move on. He was quite unmoved by anything either of us did, but he loved my pony Pud—my beautiful roan Welsh pony with his snow white rump, and would follow him quite happily anywhere he went. Not at any great speed, but faithfully in his footsteps.

We played Don Quixote and Sancho Panza several times, but we felt that this was rather a silly game. Not only because pretending to spear windmills was pointless anyway, but also because Pud being a really fat round-about, bore no resemblance at all to Rosinante. All the pictures of Rosinante were frightfully and painfully thin and bony, and I had a tiny feeling that it might be unlucky to make Pud pretend to be something so ugly, and anyway I had always hated even looking at the pictures.

When we were a little older—I was about nine I think—I decided that I would become a horse trainer. Not a race horse trainer, just to break in young horses. I was quite unafraid of horses, who seemed to like and trust me, but my wretched sister was the exact opposite. She was not only afraid of them, but they actually hated her—acting as though she was a hornet, and putting back their ears and baring their teeth when she came near. She was quite incredibly brave because she agreed to be bullied into helping me with this new venture.

I had had a certain amount of success with a young half-broken pony that I had really only taught to jump, and which I had pretended to break altogether, and one of our tenants, Paddy Cahill, seemed to be very impressed and asked if I would break in a little chestnut pony that he wanted for his mother to drive to Mass in. I was thrilled, and very confident that it would be very easy. He was a dear little pony, much smaller than the one that I had already been so successful with, and anyway, of course I could train something as small as that. Grandma christened him Darrach—Irish for Red, and his training started. He was a quiet little pony, and I drove him on a lunge for a couple of days, and then got bored with this and got on him. He was so surprised that he did nothing and I was able to ride him about quite easily. After about a week I decided that he was tame enough to begin teaching him to pull a trap. This is where Nu really showed her courage. I managed to harness Darrach without too much opposition, and—with a great deal of soothing and soft words and so on—managed to get the trap on and the traces done up. Then came the moment of moving off; Darrach plunged wildly a couple of times as he felt the trap behind him, but I held him and talked to him, and he calmed down. I then thought that he was ready to be driven.

We had wisely decided to give Darrach his first driving lesson in the Haggart, which had high walls all round, in case he happened to run away. I left Nu holding him by the head and I went round to the back and very carefully began to get into the trap. The moment that Darrach felt this awful thing apparently lifting him off his feet as the shafts lifted, he went raving mad. He plunged wildly forward, carrying Nu with him; I was thrown on my back out of the trap, and Nu, valiantly hanging on to Darrach's head, was being carried round and round the Haggart. I was yelling at her to hold on—to stop Darrach for heaven's sake or the trap would be broken or Darrach hurt. Finally she was thrown off, and Darrach careered round the Haggart twice more, the trap literally falling apart as he went, till the whole of the trap parted from the shafts, which were left hanging from the traces, and Darrach, nearly black with sweat, stood still and let me come up to him and catch him and take his harness off. It was a perfectly awful moment. There was the wrecked trap—a disaster in itself and an awful showing up of me as a failure as a trainer. Naturally, being me, I blamed it all on Nu, attacking her fiercely for not having held Darrach till I was in the trap and got the reins, but in my heart of hearts I knew that, in fact, she had come out of the whole thing better than I had.

This put our schedule of training Darrach back by about a week. But

John managed to assemble the broken trap, and by this time Darrach really was much quieter and we managed to get him to go quite well up and down the avenue several times. The only tiresome thing was that he would suddenly stop absolutely dead, while going at a fast trot, and look round behind him, trying to see round the blinkers to find out what was following him. He always went on again if I talked to him, though sometimes Nu had to lead him for a few steps.

The great day came when I decided that he was fully trained and anyway Paddy kept saying that he wanted him for his mother to go to Mass in on Easter Day. He had bought a little trap specially for the pony, and he wanted to show it off. Paddy came and saw Darrach trotting up the avenue in the donkey trap—we didn't point out the mended shafts—and he was very impressed and led him away. I was very sad to see him go, but realised that as a trainer, I would have to harden my heart to partings, and anyway, as I'd soon be inundated with new animals to train, I wouldn't have time for the ones that were ready to go.

We waited for praise from Paddy and from old Mrs Cahill, who was a bit of a tartar, and also wondered how much we should ask if he offered to pay us for the training—it was the first horse I had trained officially, so I couldn't ask too much.

A few days later the blow fell. Paddy had harnessed Darrach to the new little trap, and had proudly taken his mother to Mass. At least he had started to take his mother to Mass. When he got out on the road, (John told us what happened) there was a car passing and Darrach "went mad altogether. He ups with his heels and away with him over the wall, trap and all. His mam was thrown out on the road, and the little trap was in flitthers, no bit of it left bigger than the kippeens her Ladyship does be picking up for the fire. Ye'd better keep quiet, Miss Anne, if you do see Paddy come into the yard; 'tis red hot he is entirely. His lovely little trap all in flitthers." And John went away leaving us shaking.

We were *terrified*. Of course, we argued, Paddy was a very bad driver. Quite hopeless with a pony. He must have been driving very stupidly, but

in spite of trying to convince ourselves that he only had himself to blame, we wondered nervously whatever would he do. He never came near us, and after a week or two we stopped talking about it, and forgot to look round before we went down to the yard.

We asked John Diveney one day what had happened, and he said, "Well, Miss Anne, Paddy said it could be that a pony that would go for a lady like yourself might be afraid of a man like himself, and he had him sent to a horse-trainer near Gort, and Paddy says he's going great with him now."

"But what about the trap, John?" we asked, "was he able to mend his beautiful new trap?"

"Mend it, is it?" said John. "Sure you'd never find two bits of that trap that had ever seen the other before. Ah no, he has the new trap. I'd be thinking that himself and her Ladyship had a little bit of a talk together, and maybe Paddy thought it was better for him to get a new trap, and not be bothering yourself or Miss Catherine."

Wonderful news. We were quite safe from any unpleasantness from Paddy. We agreed that Grandma was terribly clever at talking people round. We asked her if she'd had much trouble with Paddy, and she said: "Oh well—you have to use different kinds of talk, and the different kinds work on different people."

CHAPTER X

The flower garden at Coole was one of our favourite places. About three acres, the upper part sloped down from a very high wall of grey limestone. Grandma used to push the seed pods of wallflowers into cracks in the wall, and in the spring the red and orangey wallflower made a wonderful blaze on the grey stone wall. The extraordinary thing was the number of wallflowers that grew in the wall much higher than Grandma could reach. We used to help her, but we couldn't reach very high and it was disappointing that they

57

didn't grow immediately, and when they did appear the following year, we had forgotten who had planted which ones—which annoyed us.

There were two great lengths of vineries. At the back of one, which had mainly black grapes, and where the seeds were started, there was a long shed, where all the tools were kept and at the far end of this there was a sort of pit, about 3 or 4 feet wide and about 8 feet long. At the end of this was the fire that heated the greenhouse.

Tim Gormley, the gardener, sat in here in the warmth to eat his dinner, and as he had his dinner from 12 noon to 1 o'clock, we were able to join him. He had slices of the most heavenly soda bread, with very salty butter on it. It tasted far far nicer than anything that Mary made for the house, and we used to beg slices off him. Poor Tim. He used to give us slice after slice, and it was quite delicious, and never spoilt our appetite for our own lunch at one o'clock.

It was beautifully warm sitting in this cosy pit and very hard to drag ourselves away—though when we had finished Tim's lunch we usually made off to see if there was anything exciting happening.

Tim was rather deaf, though he always seemed to understand what *we* said to him, but Grandma told us a wonderful story about a lady—an old maid, very 'wriggly and flirtatious'—who came to stay at Coole. She was English, and what with her prim way of talking and Tim being hard of hearing, he never heard a word she said.

One day she was caught in the vinery in a terrific rainstorm. Tim was in there thinning the grapes, and after a bit she yelled at him: "Gormley, I think you and I will have to spend the night here," and Tim not having heard a word, looked up at the sky and said: " 'Tis what we have all been praying for." Grandma said that she was our grandfather's cousin, and he had been in the vinery with her and heard Tim say this, and that he used to tell the story in front of her, and that she always squeaked every time he told it. We loved the thought of her squeaking, and Nu and I practised—one telling the story to an imaginary audience, and the other 'squeaking'.

The other vinery was also heated by a fire at the back, but this fire was in a definite dungeon, very dark and frightening, and about a 4 foot drop into the unknown to get there, and we never voluntarily went in. Once when the fire had gone out, we were very brave and went down with Tim to re-light it. It was very dark and dusty and much larger than we'd thought. There seemed to be all sorts of things at the far end where the light from the opening barely reached, and we were rather afraid to go and poke about to see what was hidden. We asked Tim what was there at the back, and he showed us the remains of an old still, which he said was used to make drink by gardeners at Coole who were there before himself. We asked if he ever made any, but he only shook his head and grunted, and went on poking away at the fire lighting inside the great oven.

The other frightening thing in the garden was a well in the far corner behind the laurel bushes. We had been told endlessly that we were not to go near it; that it was terribly dangerous, and that if we fell in we would drown long before anyone even heard our screams. Nu and I were far too scared to go anywhere near it at all. I wouldn't even approach the laurels that grew around it, though Nu used to make me nearly hysterical with terror by actually going up to a laurel bush and nonchalantly walking alongside it, smacking the leaves with a stick. I think the well was about 20 or 30 feet behind the great bank of bushes, but I thought she was foolhardy to a degree.

Between the vineries there was a large gravelled space, and Grandma told us that the story was that our great-great-great-grandfather had buried a pot of gold there. Several people had tried to dig it up, and one man had just got to the pot, when he looked up and saw Richard Gregory coming, and he didn't dare touch it, and ran for his life. We were thrilled, and began digging at once to find it for ourselves. We didn't get very far with our digging. The gravel was rock hard, and our spades merely made scratches on the surface. It was very frustrating. However, we decided that no-one with any sense would have bothered to bury anything under such a difficult place to make a hole, and moved our mining efforts a few yards to the side of the gravel, under the enormous yew trees that were supposed to have been grown from seed by another ancestor. We thought that it would have been more likely that a pot of gold would be buried under a tree than in the middle of a gravelled space, and anyway it was very much easier digging for us. We never found the pot of gold, though once we had a terrific thrill . . .

John Diveney and Paddy Hehir were haymaking on the tennis court and round the slopes in the flower garden, and had stopped for their tea. They were sitting in the shade on the edge of the big clump of trees on the slope. Nu and I were playing with the hay, when suddenly John shouted "Look at this Miss Anne, come here now Miss Catherine, and see what I found here in the leaves." He was rifling through the dead leaves where he was sitting, and showed us a shilling he had found under his hand. While we watched he produced another shilling and a sixpence in the same spot.

"Oh John," we yelled, "it's the treasure, let us have a go" and flung ourselves down beside him and madly began scrabbling through the leaves. At first we found nothing, then John said "try here this way a bit Miss Catherine, this might be a better place," and Nu moved slightly to her right, and at once found a sixpence. I was mad, I had found nothing.

"Where shall I search, John?" I asked frantically, "tell *me* where to look," and John sort of waved his hand over the ground, and said "I think I get the feeling of silver here, Miss Anne," as he put his hand on the ground, I began to search madly, and suddenly, through the leaves I saw the gleam of silver. A shilling! It was wonderful. John definitely must have the gift of 'feeling silver.' We went on searching and though John himself picked up another shilling, we found nothing more, though we went on searching for ages.

We went back for our tea, and told Grandma of our thrilling find nd wasn't John clever to be able to find things by magic like that, nd did Grandma think that this was really part of great-great-great-Grandpa's fortune? We were surprised and rather flattened by Grandma's obvious disbelief, and faint disapproval of our thrilling story, nd instead of dashing out herself to search for further treasure, even vent so far as to tell us that we were to give the shilling and the sixpence back to John.

"But we found them Grandma," we wailed, "we found them, hey're ours."

"You *think* you found them, Chicks," said Grandma, "but after all ohn told you exactly where to look, he must have known they were here, and so they should be his by rights. You must give them back o him," and she turned away saying something about disliking deception in any form.

Anyway, we took the money back to John, and told him that Grandma had told us to give it to him. We were quite certain that he vould say that as we had found it, it must be ours and that we should eep it, but he took it from us, just saying "That's grand. Her Ladyship knows best," as he put our lovely silver in his pocket. It was uch a horrid end to such a thrilling happening. We never saw John look-ng there again for more money, which we couldn't understand at all.

CHAPTER XI

The large clump of trees where John found the money stretched down the
slope as far as the small orchard. The apples here were all very bitter and
we never found a tree that had nice ones to eat. The trees, Ilex and ash
and beech mainly, covered about a quarter of an acre, and beyond
standing apart, was a magnificent copper beech. It was to this tree, with

s long straight trunk, that Grandma brought all the important people who stayed at Coole, to carve their names. She often showed us 'GBS' and 'Augustus John', and we actually watched Sean O'Casey carve his name. He was very good at it, and said that he had had a lot of practice, as he had often carved his name on the door of his tenement flat in Dublin. We were amazed. What an extraordinary thing to do and what on earth was a *tenement* flat?

Mr O'Casey, Grandma told us, had always lived in a Dublin slum, and didn't know what real trees were, and I can remember walking behind them down to the flower garden, the first time he came to Coole, Grandma pointing out the big chestnuts and the enormous plane tree, and telling him their names, and telling him how to distinguish the different fir trees by their shape and the shape of their fir cones. And when we got to the garden he got terribly excited at the sight of the two enormous atalpas, that Grandma told him my great-great-great-Grandfather had brought all the way back with him from one of his tours, travelling with the 10 feet high trees rolled in cloth, and carried by his servant along with all his other luggage, and finally planted them in the garden at Coole, where they had taken at once, and grown to this great size.

We had heard this story often before, so it amused us that Mr O'Casey got so excited, and he stroked the enormous leaves as though they were alive, saying that he was touching something that had travelled half across the world hundreds of years before he himself was living.

After he left, Grandma told us that she had had a lovely letter from him thanking her for his visit, and that most of it was about how beautiful the trees were at Coole, and that he had been going around the parks in Dublin looking at the trees there, seeing if he could put the names on them that he had learned at Coole . . . "but I haven't yet found the tree as fine as most of the trees are at Coole!"

Mamma used to have people to stay at Coole, who talked and talked, and who laughed a lot, but who weren't very interested in us. We were very glad about this, as grown-ups were usually very boring, and always

asked what we'd been doing during the day, and usually we didn't war
to tell them. We once told my Godmother Mrs Pope-Hennesey, who ha
seen us hurrying up from the flower garden for lunch, that we'd bee
eating Tim's lunch, and we were a bit late, as Tim had been a bit sulky a
first that day, and hadn't wanted to give us a second slice, and we wer
amazed when she told us we were selfish little cannibals and that Tir
could probably die of starvation before the day was out. We told her tha
we didn't think he would, because we knew that Blackie the cat, had ha
a very good dinner of chopped up chicken and a bit of fish, and that
Tim was really starving he'd eat that. Mrs Pope-Hennesey muttere
'selfish little savages' and obviously told Mamma, who gave us a gre
lecture on not stealing food from other people—and particularly n
from poor people like Tim, who hadn't much anyway. We hadn't stole
his food—he had given it to us—but as a result of the lecture, we used t
take some of our lunch down to Tim in an envelope each day. Stew, an
rice pudding and so on, but he always insisted that he wasn't hungry an
didn't want it—so we realised that the grown-ups were being silly again.

Dr Gogarty was one of Mamma's friends who came to Coole. We ha
been told that he was terribly witty, and told very funny stories. Nu and
kept close to the grown-ups as they walked down to the flower garde
but couldn't understand even a single joke he made. All the grown-u
laughed and laughed, but I think he was talking latin a lot of the tim
and it all seemed terribly dull. The only thing he talked about that di
thrill us, was about escaping from the Sinn Feiners. Apparently he ha
been kidnapped by a band of the Sinn Feiners, who had kept him in
house on the banks of the Liffey. One evening when one of them brougl
him his supper, he had knocked him out and had rushed through the doc
of the house before the rest realised what had happened and thre
himself into the Liffey, and had swum downstream—under water—fc
miles. The Sinn Feiners had run along the bank shooting at him wheneve
he put his head up to get air ". . . but all they hit was a swan that wa
swimming beside me when I came up, and they were so excited at getting

wan that they forgot about me, and I was able to swim down to Dublin."
Roars of appreciation from the grown-ups, but Nu and I were secretly
distressed. How *awful* shooting a swan—and apart from killing a swan, it
was terrible unlucky too. We looked with distaste at Dr Gogarty and
thought he shouldn't have swum so near to a swan to make it so
dangerous for it—it was a mean trick.

A few years later Dr Gogarty took my tonsils out in Dublin, with a
local anaesthetic. After the first tonsil was out, a nurse came in with a
telegram. Dr Gogarty looked at it and said it was for me and that I had
better read it in case it was urgent. I sat up on the operating table
covered in blood, and read that Richard had done marvellously well in
his Army Entrance Exam, having passed among the first ten. I was
pleased, but very disappointed that it wasn't something more dramatic,
that might have released me from the operating room. So I had to lie
down, and have the second tonsil removed. It was all very unpleasant,
and later on that day, when I nearly bled to death from a haemorrhage
from the throat, I thought of the swan episode and was furious that
though Dr Gogarty had been responsible for the death of the swan, it
looked as though the bad luck was coming to me, and that *I* was going to
die for it.

The Gogartys had a lovely house in Connemara, Renvyle, and we went
over there once or twice in a motor car. These were some of the first
journeys we had ever had in a car, and it was all very thrilling. The model
' Ford was a wonderful car, and covered the ground at an enormous
speed. I didn't mind how fast we went, but going slowly up steep hills
filled me with terror. I was quite convinced that we were going to roll
backwards down the hill, and however much the grown-ups told me that
this couldn't happen, I was never really reassured and every trip we made
would be ruined for me if there was a steep hill to negotiate on the way.

I had a sort of feeling that if I kept on reciting poetry out loud, nothing awful would happen—like the car rolling backwards, and from the
moment we left the safety of the avenue and got on the road, I would

begin droning all the verses I knew by heart. Grandma always gave u
poems to learn, and I had enough poetry to last for nearly an hou
without repetition—from 'Lars Porsena of Clusium' and 'The Assyria
came down like a wolf on the fold' to short ones like 'We are the Musi
Makers'.

Mamma always thought that I was reciting out loud because I love
driving in the car so much, she never knew it was an incantation to kee
trouble from destroying us all. However, we usually got safely t
wherever we were going, though we did have a lot of punctures.

Once when we went to Renvyle, Augustus John was painting Brenda
Dr Gogarty's daughter. We didn't think much of her at the time, an
were very disgusted at the fuss everyone was making over the picture.

Brenda—we thought—was very ugly, but she had the most marvellou
coloured blue eyes, and the picture was very odd. It had a sort o
sketched-in face and arm, and two brilliant blue eyes, completely painted
and standing out like a couple of pieces of the sky. Nu and I merel
thought it looked odd and unfinished, though we could recognise Brend
from the eyes; but everyone seemed to be talking together about it t
Augustus John, and some were saying one thing and so on. I remembe
Mamma telling him that it was far and away the best thing he had eve
done, *if* he left it alone and never laid another stroke on it, and Joh
getting very snappy, and saying something about "well I might leave th
head, but that arm looks as though she's had a stroke, as well as having
man's hand at the end of it. Whatever else, I can't leave *that* as it is," an
Mamma said "Oh, if you touch it at all you won't be able to leave any o
it alone, and you'll spoil the whole thing as you always do." And Joh
stamped off—we couldn't hear what he said, but Mamma told u
afterwards that he had done exactly as she had said at the time, and ha
virtually repainted the whole picture, and it was now just an ordinar
picture, and not the fantastic thing it had been. Nu and I were quit
pleased to hear that Brenda wasn't going to be the subject of John's bes
work.

I had a bit of a crush on Dermot, one of Dr Gogarty's sons, and he sent me a rather snubbing letter about something. I decided to get even with him. I had a brilliant idea. I waited till Mike John shot a rabbit, and gutted it, and then I put all the horrible insides in a cardboard box, and made a very neat parcel of it—it looked rather an exciting parcel, like a box of chocolates or something—and sent it off addressed to Dermot, and was thrilled thinking of his horror when he unwrapped it at breakfast the next day.

Nu told Mamma what I had done, and Mamma was horrified. She told Nu she was to take the car at once, she *must* take the car or she'd miss the post, and dash into Gort two miles away before the post went. It was the power of Mamma's voice and personality that caused Nu to rush out and do as she was told without hesitation. She took the car, drove to Gort—she told me afterwards—with the accelerator lever hard down the whole way, hit nothing, and got the parcel before the post left, which she brought back for Mamma to destroy. And she had never even driven a car in her life before!

67

CHAPTER XII

It was because of illness that I learned to drive.

The local doctor had been coming daily to see Grandma who had had an operation, and one day I asked him if I might drive his car to the White Gate. He didn't mind and we had a pleasant drive, chattering away about this and that, while we went along at a splendid pace. When we got to the White Gate, I got out and opened it for him, and he beamed at me and said: "You drive very well for your age (I was rising twelve at the time), who taught you?"

"No one," says I, "I've never driven a car before." Dr Coyne nearly fainted, and dashed through the gate; but he was very kind and let me drive his car to the White Gate every day he came, though he did suggest that I went a bit more slowly than I'd done the first time.

I wrote off to Galway for a licence, not giving my age, nor the fact that I hadn't yet driven on the public road, and wrote on Coole notepaper signing myself Augusta Anne Gregory, which is my name. By return of post came my driving licence, with a note inside. "I hope your Ladyship will have many happy days driving through the countryside." I didn't tell anyone that the office had obviously thought that it was Grandma who had applied for the licence—her name being Augusta too—and I was thrilled to have the licence, because now I really could drive anywhere without fear of the law.

The biggest hazards on the roads were the endless hens feeding outside every cottage, which were quite half-witted when they saw the car, and dashed backwards and forwards under the wheels, and the collie dogs which appeared like magic from over the walls as well as out of the cottages when they heard the car. They were really very frightening these dogs. They'd rush in front of the car, thinking that by barking in front of it it would stop and turn, like the sheep and cattle they were used to herding. And it was horribly difficult to get past them; and as soon as one had managed to manoeuvre past, leaving one dog barking madly behind in a cloud of dust, another would rush out from somewhere, and the whole thing would start all over again.

One day—not long after I'd got my licence—Grandma, who took it for granted that one could learn to drive a car as easily as driving a pony, said that we'd drive into Co. Clare to pick up a cousin of mine for a short visit to Coole. This was a great thrill because Maurice was very handsome, with flashing black eyes, and I thought he was marvellous; and the big thrill was that though he was several years older than me, he couldn't drive a car. This was the day when he was going to notice me.

The drive to Corofin was uneventful, and the Model T went beautifully and we didn't get a puncture; and though the Studderts seemed slightly horrified at me being allowed to drive, I merely took this as a compliment.

On the way back, with Grandma and Nu sitting in the back and with the marvellous Maurice sitting beside me, I felt quite dizzy with importance, and was determined to show this glamorous cousin how splendidly I could handle our chariot. I pulled the accelerator lever down farther and farther—never had I gone as fast as this. Even the dogs seemed to recognise that it was no good trying to herd this apparition, and the dust rose high and enveloped us, and we seemed to be sailing along in a cloud. We flew over the bumps, the Ford making light work of them, and we came to a hump backed bridge. We had crossed it coming, but I didn't realise the difference that speed would make, and the Ford took off and bucked like a wild animal, before I could get her straight on the road. For a moment no one spoke. Then rather shakily I said to Maurice: "I kept her quite straight on the road didn't I?" expecting an admiring answer, when there was a frantic wail from Nu in the back.

"Anne—stop, stop—you've killed Grandma. You've killed her. She's pouring with blood."

I pulled up—rather resentfully—and there was Grandma, huddled up on the back seat, her face in her hands and blood pouring in a stream on to her lap. It was awful. Grandma had been bounced up over the bump, and had hit her face on the bar of the hood, and was nearly unconscious, with her nose and mouth pouring with blood. I felt doubly shattered. Not only had I done this to Grandma by driving too fast over the bump, but also I had shown Maurice that I wasn't really such a good driver. Grandma put one hand in her bag, and pulled out a handkerchief which she held over her face.

"I'm all right," she said. "I'm quite all right. Drive on home."

It was a nightmare drive. I was torn between wild anxiety about Grandma, rocking herself backwards and forwards in the back, with little groans that I could hear now and then, and trying to justify myself and my driving to Maurice.

"I can't *think* why Grandma went so high in the air, she must have been sitting forward to say something just when we came to that bridge," I said, "it wasn't such a terrific bump really, she *must* have been sitting in an odd position."

"You were driving much too fast," said Maurice, "that was the only reason."

The scales fell from my eyes. This man was nothing but mortal.

Grandma sent John for the doctor as soon as we got home, and he came at once. Grandma had broken her nose, and for days she had a horrible plaster over it; she had also broken her teeth, but they were mended more easily and quicker than her nose.

She never told Mamma or anyone what had happened, or that it had been entirely my fault. She never suggested even that I should learn to drive properly before I went on the main road again, but she gave me a serious lecture about showing-off, and then never mentioned it or her poor sore nose again.

During the war, we used to have either butter or jam on our bread, but not both together, "to help the troops" Grandma told us. G.B.S. stayed with us one time when we were 'rationed' like this. Nu and I often had tea with the grown-ups in the breakfast-room, and we were very horrified one day when we both noticed G.B.S. buttering his slice of bread, and then turning it over and asking us to pass him the jam ... "as I've no butter on my bread." We pretended not to hear, and when Grandma sharply told us to pass the jam to G.B.S. we tried to signal her with our eyes and grimaces that something awful was going on. She didn't seem to understand, and of

71

course we couldn't say anything out loud. When we'd finished tea and were on our own, we discussed what we could do, but decided that really there was nothing. We couldn't sneak, but we would try to shame him by staring at him the whole time. G.B.S. seemed quite unaware of our hostile eyes boring into him and continued serenely to butter his bread, and then turn it over for jam.

Not very long after this we went to England, and Grandma sent us lovely Coóle butter every week, carefully packed in the covers of a book. We were thrilled both by the butter, which tasted quite different from any other butter we had ever tasted, and also by the clever way that Grandma had cut the pages out of the book, and fitted the butter exactly into the cover.

CHAPTER XIII

Christmas at Coole. Such a lovely time. Every year John Quinn, Grandma's great friend in New York, used to send a great case of apples to us. One year they were red and the next green. They were so marvellous, because although Grandma always stored a lot of apples from our trees, they were nearly always a bit wrinkled by Christmas, and were never brilliant and shiny like the ones from Mr Quinn.

He also sent us the biggest boxes of sweets we had ever seen—they were round boxes, and far far too large for us to get our arms around. We always tried to put our arms around the box to make sure that they really were as big as we had remembered them the year before. Dear John Quinn. We never met him, but he never forgot us year after year.

Every time that Grandma went to America with the Abbey Players, she always visited John Quinn, and I'm sure she passed on our messages to him about the apples and sweets.

Going to church on Christmas day was always more exciting. Two Irish miles each way—usually in the Victoria—but if it was really very wet we went in the brougham. The brougham was very heavy for Cobje to pull, and also it wasn't nearly so nice to ride in. It was more bumpy, and much more smelly than the Victoria, which was a lovely carriage, and you couldn't see out nearly so well.

Grandma always had about twenty little parcels with her to give to people at Church, and one or two to people in Crow Lane; when we stopped in the Lane, a small crowd of children always gathered from nowhere, and stared at the Coole carriage standing there. Nu and I were rather embarrassed by this and wished that Grandma wouldn't talk for so long to the people who came out of their cottages for their presents.

Gort church was fun, because the Gregorys and the Goughs had two private balconies facing each other across the aisle. The Gregorys had to walk across the church to go up their private stairs, but the Goughs didn't have to come into the church at all; their staircase led up from the outer door, so we never knew if there was anyone in their pew till we got to the top of our staircase. Nu and I had a theory that they weren't really in church where they sat, as they hadn't had to come into church to get there.

Grandma sat next to the wall in her armchair—we all had arm chairs, unlike the Goughs who had two arm chairs for Lord and Lady Gough, and everyone else had straight chairs, rather like in a dining-room,—and Nu sat between Grandma and me. Grandma didn't kneel down, only leaned forward in her chair to say her prayers, and we used to try to copy her, which was very uncomfortable. But Grandma told us that she used to kneel till her knees got too stiff, and that we must do the same all our life till *we* got too stiff, and then it wouldn't be impertinent of us to stay sitting in our chairs. She had a very special prayer book, with

74

lovely brass bindings, and sometimes she leant over to show us what page we should be looking at. Her prayer book was numbered quite differently from the ones we were using and so it was terribly difficult to follow.

We always had an enormous Christmas tree, even if we were on our own. Grandma would mark a tree early in the year, as the one we were going to have, and it was kept specially free from grass and ivy so that it wouldn't grow lop-sided. It was always put up in the breakfast room late on Christmas eve, and Grandma and Mamma decorated it after lunch on Christmas day. We weren't allowed to see it, either before or after it was decorated until we were called in—wild with excitement—when all the candles were alight. The room looked like fairyland with the silver star glittering at the tip-top of the enormous tree, nearly touching the ceiling; the candles flickering made all the pictures on the walls appear to move with the light coming and going on the glass; the masses of piled parcels at the base of the tree, and masses more little parcels in bright paper tied on the branches among the fairylike decorations; and above all, the wonderful heady smell of hot candlegrease.

We never started opening our presents till we had gone round and round the tree, drinking in the beauty, making certain that all the old decorations were on and asking Grandma how on *earth* she had managed to climb up and put the star on the top. Then we'd go round and round again to see if we could see our names on the labels, and then we looked for our presents to each other, which we'd handed over to Grandma earlier to be hung on the tree with the rest of the presents.

Finally, we got down to the great opening of presents, each of us sitting in a special place, with Grandma sitting in the centre, opening her presents and exclaiming over each one that we had given her, that it was the one thing she had hoped she would get, that it was beautifully made—we always made our presents to Mamma and Grandma—and we all felt so pleased with ourselves that we had been so clever.

75

On St. Stephen's day—Boxing Day visitors used to call it—the Wren boys came. The Wren boys, Grandma told us, always killed a wren on this day, and went around with its little body on a stick, because years ago, when the Irish were about to encircle a camp of English invaders, a wren began pecking at some crumbs on a drum belonging to an English sentry, and woke him up, and he gave the alarm and the Irish were driven off, and many of them killed. And in this way they warned the wren not to do such a thing again. But Grandma always told the Wren boys that if she saw them with a dead wren, or if she heard that anyone of them had killed one, she would give them nothing ever again, and so we never saw a little body. The Wren boys blacked their faces, and dressed in the most odd clothes. Usually they seemed to have women's skirts, and strange things on their heads. Grandma said that they were pretending to be the invading army that was beaten off, and in those days they wore odd clothes, and also were in disguise when they attacked. Although they wore skirts, there was never a girl among them, but their heavy nailed boots never looked strange to us, because all the girls we saw wore the self-same boots on Sundays.

Grandma kept a heap of small apples for the Wren boys, and when each troop of Wren boys had performed their turn of songs and dance, which varied slightly, but which had to finish with:

> The wran the wran, the King of all Birds,
> St. Stephens day was cot in the Furze,
> Although he is small his family's great,
> Rise up kind lady and give us a trate.
>
> We followed him for a mile or more
> We followed him to Coole front door,
> Up with the kettle, down with the pan,
> Give us a penny to bury the wran.

she'd give the leader a few coppers, and then with cries of 'scib-scab, scib-scab' she'd throw handfuls of apples along the gravel, and the Wren boys madly rushed after them, fighting and scrambling to get as many as they could, heaving up their skirts to put what they couldn't carry into the pockets of their breeks underneath. The scuffles often continued away down the drive, as the more successful were set upon by their less lucky or less active friends.

One Christmas Nu and I dressed up as Wren boys.

We decided that we must have someone else with us, as Grandma would certainly be suspicious of just two small Wren boys by themselves, and decided on Mike John because we knew that we could probably talk him into doing it, and he had a mouth organ he used to play sometimes.

Mike John wasn't very keen at first, but we managed to persuade him, promising that we would find him clothes that Grandma wouldn't recognise him in. Mike John then agreed to get the blackening for our faces, and we arranged to meet in the barn to dress up.

We raided the camphor chests in the long passage and found two long grown-ups' skirts for ourselves, but sadly discarded two beautiful lacey blouses because Wren boys always wore old coats turned inside out, or pink or purple shiny blouses, but *never* lacey ones. At the bottom of the chest we found a wonderful red petticoat, which was perfect for Mike John, and a very long red and white woollen scarf that he could wear inside the neck of his old mackintosh.

But what about his head?

Nu and I had decided we'd wear old shooting hats pulled right down over our ears, but Mike John always wore a hat like that, and anyway—even though his face was black—his droopy moustache would show.

We wandered down to the cloakroom and gazed round the odd coats and sticks and things.

"We *must* find something that he can pull down right over his face to

77

hide his moustache" I said to Nu for the twentieth time, "Grandma will see it at once otherwise."

We gazed up at the pegs where the hats were hanging—and a great light dawned. The marvellous answer to our problem was staring at us. Of *course*! Grandma's hats always had a small veil, and if Mike John wore one tipped forward a bit, it would be perfect.

We looked at each other a shade apprehensively. Would Grandma be very cross?

"Well," said Nu stoutly, "I don't think she'll recognise it anyway. It will look *quite* different on Mike John."

We looked again at the hats. Grandma always left her everyday hat in the cloakroom, but today—on the next peg—was the hat she'd worn at Church the day before. She must have forgotten to take it upstairs. It was a lovely hat—black of course, like all her hats—with little satin rosettes round the band, and a very good veil—about two inches long with spots on it, hanging all the way round from the brim.

"We can't take her *Sunday* hat," I protested—very weakly because I knew it would suit Mike John so well—"she'd be *furious* if we took her *Sunday* hat."

"Well," said Nu, "we can't take her everyday hat because she'll want to put it on when the Wren boys come, but as she won't be wearing her Sunday hat till next Sunday, she won't miss that."

I glowered at Nu. How maddening of her to have thought of that. I should have thought of it first. After all, I was the oldest.

We took Grandma's spud from the elephant-foot stand, and stretching on tiptoe managed to hook the Sunday hat off its peg, then gathering up all the clothes we had left in a heap in the tiny dining-room, we scampered down to the barn.

Mike John *was* waiting—and we were rather relieved, because we thought that he might easily not be there—grown-ups were sometimes very forgetful. He had already blacked his face, and looked very comic.

We gave him the red petticoat and scarf, and told him to put his

78

old mackintosh on inside out. The petticoat was much too small round his waist, but he tied an old piece of rope round it to keep it from falling off. When he had put on the mac and the red and white scarf he looked marvellous. He put on his hat.

"Oh *No*, Mike John," we said, "you can't wear your own hat,

Grandma would know you at once; we have brought you a much better one than yours," and we produced the hat with great pride. "Here you are Mike John," we said, "Grandma will never know you in this," and we gave it to him.

Mike John took the hat and held it in his hand; he looked very shocked.

"That's one of her Ladyship's hats," he gasped, " 'twouldn't be right for me to put on one of *them*."

Nu and I assured him that Grandma wouldn't mind—that she wouldn't recognise it; but he remained absolutely firm.

"No, Miss Anne," he said, "indeed no, Miss Catherine, it wouldn't be right."

Bother Mike John. He was going to spoil everything. He simply *must* hide his moustache under that veil.

"But Grandma doesn't *ever* wear this hat," we lied firmly, "she put it in the old clothes basket at the end of the long passage where she puts all her old clothes for dressing scarecrows. It's going to be thrown away anyway. You *must* wear it, Mike John." Finally we persuaded him that what we said was true, and he put on the hat.

It was *marvellous* . . . worth all our lies. You couldn't possibly tell who he was—and it did look quite different on Mike John.

We heard one lot of Wren boys singing up at the house, and when we saw them making off down the avenue, we walked brazenly up to the front door, doing a sort of scuffling hop skip and dance that we'd seen the other Wren boys doing, and Mike John played a tune on his mouth organ.

"We'll begin *and* end with the 'Wran' " I said bossily, "Grandma loves 'the Wran', and we'll sing 'Kevin Barry' next, and then we'll give a step of a dance while Mike John plays a jig."

We banged on the front door good and hard, and began singing 'The Wran, the Wran' at the top of our voices. Grandma must have been in the breakfast room because she appeared almost at once. Nu and I nudged each other appreciatively. Grandma was wearing her everyday hat. *What* a bit of luck we hadn't borrowed it.

We finished two verses of 'The Wran'—stamped and shuffled our feet as the Wren boys always did between tunes—then broke into 'Kevin Barry', the song about the young man who was tortured by the British in his lonely prison cell. Mike John stood slightly in front of us, playing away on his mouth organ—we didn't know what tune he was playing because we couldn't hear him above our own voices singing—but Grandma obviously thought we were very good, because we could see that she was smiling and nodding, which she always did when the Wren boys were singing well. When we had finished 'Kevin Barry'—the last few lines invented because we couldn't remember them all—we hissed "play the jig Mike John" and flung ourselves energetically into one of the dances Sister Columba had tried to teach us at the Convent. Now we felt we could do it just like Sister Columba did, because our skirts were down to the ground like hers, and what a difference that made. We were marvellous—never a mistake—but we had to bang Mike John on the back to stop him before we were quite exhausted. We managed to pant through two more verses—the same ones actually—of 'The Wran, the Wran' and Grandma was obviously very pleased as she beckoned us to come and get our money.

We pushed Mike John forward; Grandma would be certain to recognise us close up, and we *did* want to hear her saying afterwards how good this lot of Wren boys had been.

Mike John stepped forward, and Grandma began thanking him for the splendid recital, and was about to put what *looked* like two half-crowns into his hand.

Two half-crowns?

Grandma only ever gave pennies—and now and again a sixpence when they sang specially well. But two half-crowns! We really must have been absolutely marvellous. Nu and I nodded congratulations at each other, then suddenly our tummies turned over . . . Grandma—her hand still held out with the money in it—looked up at Mike John and gave a great gasp.

"Mike John," she said in a furious voice, "*Where* did you get that hat?"

Mike John shuffled. He said nothing.

"Did you take that hat out of the cloakroom?" Grandma asked him.

"I did not then, My Lady, you know well I'd not do a thing like that . . . sure wasn't it lying in the old linen basket it was, waiting to dress a scarecrow, and there's no harm done to it at all, at all," and he took the hat from his head and handed it to Grandma, who took it with two fingers, and turned and carried it at arm's length into the house.

Mike John gave a furious grunt.

"Bad cess to the two of ye then," he said as he passed us, "her Ladyship will skin ye for giving me her Sunday-go-meeting hat, and she'll likely kill me for putting it on," and he went off towards the barn, muttering under his breath, and looking very odd with his black face and naked-looking white head.

Nu and I crept in the back way, pulling off our Wren boy clothes as we went. What on earth would Grandma say to us? We washed the black off our faces in the pantry—very thankful that Marian was over in her room, and hadn't seen all that was going on—and went through to the hall.

Horror!

Grandma's hat was on the floor in the middle of the hall. She must have just dropped it there and left it. This was awful. She must be really terribly angry to drop something on the floor and leave it there.

We decided to go up to the nursery and say nothing. Perhaps she hadn't recognised us, as we hadn't come very close to her.

The astonishing thing was that Grandma never mentioned the Wren boys who had sung and danced so well, and never said a word about her hat or Mike John, so Nu and I decided that it would be very silly of us to bring up the subject. But the extraordinary thing was that we never saw the hat again till the summer, and then—we could hardly believe our eyes—it was on the scarecrow!

CHAPTER XIV

When Sean O'Casey was staying with us, John Diveney met him at the station in the side car, and drove him out. I don't know what they talked about, but Nu and I could tell from John's look as he took his little case from the well of the car, that he was disapproving of something. We were watching with great interest because Grandma had told us that Mr O'Casey was going to be one of the most talked about Irish playwrights of the century, and we wanted to see what the people would be talking about. Marian went to the door to let him in, and her "Welcome to Coole" died on her lips and we could see a look of utter disbelief on her face as she gazed at Mr O'Casey.

We craned out of the nursery window, fascinated, trying to see what had surprised Marian. Gazing down all we could see was a bare greyish head and his shoulders in a rather shabby grey overcoat. What on *earth* was she looking at? We dashed down the back stairs and waited for Marian to come into the pantry. We could hear her muttering as she came down from the drawing-room.

"What's he like, Marian?" we asked tactfully, "What does the great playwright look like?"

"Great *playwright* is it?" Marian snorted, drawing herself up, her starched apron creaking, her white cap quivering with fury. "Great *playwright*? I'll give him great *playwright*. What *right* at all has a man like that to come into Coole without a tie on his collar, nor a collar on his shirt."

We were entranced. "What did Grandma say to him?" we asked, "Did Grandma notice?"

"Indeed and she noticed," said Marian, "and why wouldn't she? But her Ladyship wouldn't let a tinker know he stank, let alone had he slept all night in the sty. She said the same as she always says, 'You're welcome to Coole, Mr O'Casey,' she said 'Cead mille failthe to you, Mr O'Casey,' and she shook him by the hand the same as she'd welcome a lady or a gentleman, but if that man comes into the dining-room with the bare neck showing, I'll give him great playwright, so I will."

Nu and I were thrilled, but we knew Marian and her rages, which were every bit as much bite as bark, so when Grandma was changing for dinner, we crept up to her room and told her what Marian had said.

"It's unkind of Marian to talk like that," Grandma said, "Mr

84

O'Casey is a very poor man, and she shouldn't be down on him because he hasn't the price of a tie," but we heard her go along to Mr O'Casey's room on her way downstairs. We asked her afterwards what he had said, and Grandma said that he quite understood and that he didn't want to appear discourteous to Grandma, and he tied a 'neckchief' around his neck. Grandma said that though it wasn't exactly a collar and tie at least his bare white neck was covered, and Marian did hand him his food, though standing well back from him as she did so!

We were both fascinated by him, for though Grandma had told us about him having taught himself to read and write, and that he had written such a brilliant play, we hadn't realised that he would have such a terrific Dublin accent. We couldn't believe that anyone who talked like that could write much at all, let alone write brilliant plays, and we listened intently as he and Grandma talked and talked over lunch and tea.

Mr O'Casey seemed to get very worked up about slums and class and this seemed to us a very tactless thing to attack Grandma about—it wasn't *her* fault, she was always trying to help poor people and never made any difference in the way she talked to anyone, and wouldn't let us talk differently to anyone either—but Grandma listened to all he was saying, and then agreed with him, and said it was unfair, but that it was only someone like himself that had the gift of words who could show the other side what living in slums was really like. We were a bit bothered by the 'other side' bit. We thought that the 'other side' meant Heaven, and surely Heaven should know how Mr O'Casey lived already.

Anyway, Grandma told Mr O'Casey that it was useless—worse than useless to try to get better houses and better jobs with guns ... "because only frightened people use guns, and no-one wants to live near frightened people, nor give them jobs, because they know that they may use guns again at any minute" ... Mr O'Casey argued passionately about this, but Nu and I asked if we could be excused, because it seemed a very dull conversation, and we had more exciting things to do.

* * *

As I was born in September and Nu in August, we were always down in Burren for our birthdays. Grandma used to come for the day; it was simply wonderful. She'd arrive on the side-car in time for lunch, the well absolutely stuffed with food from Coole—late gooseberries, masses of raspberries, strawberries, masses of different vegetables, some early apple windfalls, chickens, plucked and unplucked, and several rabbits. On Nu's birthday Grandma usually managed to bring at least one bunch of grapes that was anyway *nearly* ripe. It would have been a disaster if there hadn't been at least one bunch ripe enough to bring. Grandma used to say "I had great difficulty in ripening that bunch in time, but there will be a lot ready for Annekin's birthday." We wondered how she ripened the special bunch, but she never told us how she did it.

Grandma always made some special thing each year, to put on top of the birthday cake, always a splendid sight—enormous—made by Mary at Coole and beautifully iced. It was always a sponge cake with a couple of layers of jam inside. But Grandma cut out (in cardboard) some figure or decoration to sit on top of the cake, that made each one quite different.

I can remember the thrill of one that was on my cake on my tenth birthday. I had been given a gun for Christmas, and had shot several rabbits, and two roosting pigeons with it in the winter. The decoration on my cake was a cut-out of me standing with my gun at my shoulder pointing at a tree with a bird on it, and a rabbit sitting up at my feet saying, "That's right dear, always aim high," and Grandma said that Jack Yeats had drawn it for her to copy, but she had cut out the little sketch and stuck it on cardboard, and coloured both sides. It really was very beautiful.

Grandma stayed with us till about 4 o'clock, and had a cup of tea before she left, and then set out again for Coole. She always said the journey to Burren seemed very short because she was so excited at the thought of seeing her 'chicks' and the journey home seemed very short because Cobje knew he was on his way home, and went very fast all the way.

Jack Yeats used to come to Coole now and again, but I don't remember him being there as often as W.B. who stayed there nearly all the time. He painted such lovely pictures, Jack Yeats did, and Grandma got him to draw two pictures of Nu and me. Me on Pud cantering up the slope on the front lawn, with Taddy, my little terrier bouncing up at Pud's nose as he always did, and Nu sitting very peacefully on Tommy just in front of the house. We were very pleased with these pictures, though I was sorry that Taddy didn't show up a bit better, and Nu was a bit sad that Tommy was standing still, and not galloping like Pud; but I said to her "you are lucky that Mr Yeats didn't paint you standing on the ground just beating Tommy, trying to make him *walk*."

One of the most marvellous pictures of his we ever saw was the enormous one in a red frame, in Richard's room. It was painted on a sort of cardboard, and was of a boy in torn trousers and a magnificent hat with a plume in it, on a splendid horse, with an arched neck and flowing mane, riding along the sea shore with a ship on the sea in the background. It was a Christmas card he had sent Richard, and underneath was written to R. 'Youthful Theodore'.

We had no idea why on earth it was called Youthful Theodore if it was meant to be our brother, because *his* name was Richard. So we asked Mamma and she said that: "Youthful Theodore was *always* courteous to the ladies" which still made little sense to us, though we adored the picture. I was terribly jealous actually, as *I* was the one who rode a lot, and Richard really liked mechanical things better, but perhaps he had liked horses more when the picture was painted.

We had several of Mr Yeats' pictures. There was a wonderful rolling donkey. The donkey was rolling in the middle of a dusty road, and was on its back. I remember Mamma saying that it was the most difficult way to paint a donkey. I was rather worried by it because I kept feeling that some dreadful car might come along and run into it. There were also some lovely stencils in the hall that he had done. All sporting pictures. One was of a boxer, and another of a man running in a race. They were very clever, as they were done in sort of lines, through the cut-out paper he had made—at least that is how Grandma told us he had done them. They hung on the wall over about six glass cases that had different birds in them. There was one case that had a marten cat in it that had been shot at Coole. Apparently it was the last marten cat ever seen in Ireland. Further along on the wall were various glass frames with pieces of stone with writing on them from Nineveh, and there was a long piece of wood, that was a bit of flagstaff.

There was a note stuck on it, which was rather faded, but was very exciting to read as it said:

"Headquarters Dept. of S.C.
Charleston S.C. Febry. 10. 1864
"Piece of Flagstaff of Fort Sumter of Charleston, sent with my compliments to Hon Wm. H. Gregory M.P. for Galway.

"The flagstaff of this Fort has already been shot down over forty times by the enemy's fire since the commencement of the siege July 10th 1863.

G. T. Beauregard

Genl. U.S.A."

we thought it marvellous that this was really a bit of the actual flagstaff that had been shot down so often, and were rather annoyed that Grandma wouldn't let us borrow it for one of our camps, which we defended—equally bravely—against the Indians.

There were also mummy cases from Nineveh or somewhere, which looked like some sort of little stone animals sitting up and begging. The hall floor was all small different coloured tiles in patterns, and it was on to this terrible hard floor that Grandma had fallen down the stairs that dreadful time.

CHAPTER XV

One day when Marian was away on an almost unprecedented holiday, Ellen told us that she had taken Mr Yeats his early morning tea to his room, ". . . and there he was, sitting up in bed, with two jerseys on over his nightshirt, and a suit on over that, and his top coat over his shoulders and a woolly scarf tied round his head, like as if he was walking the woods at night." We were thrilled, what a wonderful sight he must be. We asked

Ellen again to give us exact details of what he really looked like, but it was so desperately frustrating, because of course we couldn't go into his room while he was in bed. However, we crept in later on when Ellen was making his bed, very much on edge in case he came up from his breakfast and found us there, and asked Ellen to show us all the things he'd been wearing. She showed us the nightshirt—of thick flannel—then picked up a pyjama jacket from the bed.

"Sure, he must have had these on under the shirt," she exclaimed, "I never saw the payjames on him at all. And where now are the trousies?" We couldn't find the 'trousies' and Ellen said she reckoned he had them on still.

"Which suit did he have on?" we whispered, not daring to speak out loud. "Show us the suit . . . and the scarf," we added urgently. "Oh hurry *up* Ellen." Ellen went to the cupboard.

"Aah, he must be wearing the self-same suit at the breakfast," she said, "it's not here in the closet . . . but that's the muffler he had around his neck right enough," and she showed us a pale blue woollen scarf on the back of the chair.

"Which were the jerseys, Ellen? where are the jerseys?" . . . but maddeningly we heard sounds of voices downstairs, and the breakfast room door opening, and we dashed out. It would have been *awful* if we'd been seen in Mr Yeats's room.

At lunch, when we saw Mr Yeats, we looked closely at his suit, and decided that it really must have been the suit he slept in—it was certainly very baggy and creased. We tried to see if there was any sign of his pyjama trousies appearing below his trousers, but couldn't see anything.

We looked on Mr Yeats with much more respect after this—to be able to do such an extraordinary thing at Coole, and not appear to mind, was marvellous; but we never told Grandma as we thought she might be shocked, and anyway, she was always asking Marian if she had taken up Mr Yeats' bottle to his bed, and she might think that Ellen had forgotten it this night.

Grandma used to have terrible chilblains on her hands, and we knitted her endless wristlets which she wore and said that they were wonderful for keeping out the cold; but she got Marian to knit her mittens, which she wore nearly all the year round. Sometimes when she'd been out picking up kippeens, they got dripping wet, and she hung them to dry on the curly tops of the fire dogs in the library, where she hung her handkerchief in the evening when she was reading Uncle Remus. If it was tea time, though, she hung them on the brass fender, and the steam rose like a cloud as Nu and I made our toast. Nu and I kept on feeling them as we squatted with our toasting forks in front of the fire, telling Grandma that they were dry, and Grandma felt them and said, "No, they're done on one side, like your toast—turn them over and cook the other side." And in time they dried and Grandma put them on again, all warm and rather crisp.

Grandma loved toast hot from the fire, and we always made it piece by piece, eating each piece as it was ready before we did the next slice. Grandma sat on a chair, holding her toasting fork to the middle of the fire, and Nu and I squatted on the floor either side of her, often looking enviously at the other, where the fire looked much hotter than our own place. Lovely flickering light from the fire played all over us, and on the brass fender and on the underside of the great mantelpiece. Sometimes it got too hot and Grandma held her handkerchief in front of her face, and we'd say, "Is your handkerchief clean Grandma?" and she'd say: "What is it a rich man puts in his pocket and a poor man throws away?" And though we knew the answer very well, we always asked: "We give it up, Grandma, what's the answer?" and she'd say: "A rich man . . ." and pretend to blow her nose in her handkerchief, and tuck it in an imaginery trouser pocket, ". . . and a poor man . . ." and she'd pretend to blow her nose with her fingers, and we'd scream with laughter at the sort of disdainful way she did it, and sometimes we forgot that we were toasting our bread, and the slice fell in the fire, and chaos reigned till it was safely—if rather sootily—recovered.

Grandma walked a lot. Round the gardens, and usually all through the Nut wood, but if she was going to the farther away woods, Parc na Carragh, the Isabella or towards Inchy, she'd go in the donkey trap. Tommy was a dear kind donkey, but not very interested in what went on, and he wandered along as slowly as he could. When we went with Grandma we could make him trot now and again with the use of a great deal of screaming "go on outa that," and the use of ash sticks, which raised a great deal of dust from his fur, but which he treated with a certain amount of disdain. Grandma never used a stick on him. She had a spud, which she carried everywhere with her, partly as a walking stick, but she loved to attack thistles and nettles growing near her beloved young trees, and she used this spud to prod Tommy whenever he stopped in his tracks; now and again he must have felt it, as Grandma always got to where she wanted in the wood, and of course once he was headed for home, there was no need for a goad.

There was one time, which I don't remember personally, but which Grandma often retailed with great relish, when she took Count de Basterot with her to see the great rocks in the Isabella wood. Count de Basterot talked and talked and never drew breath, and Tommy went slower and slower and Grandma thought they'd never get to Fox-rock and when they finally got there, Grandma said: "These are the famous rocks, they are supposed to be older than any other known rocks in Galway—we'll turn for home now," and turned Tommy round and gave him a great jab with her spud. As she did this Tommy apparently spun round like a top, and set off for home at a terrific gallop. Grandma was so astonished that she had to hang on to the reins and for hundreds of yards was unable to listen to the Count. When Tommy eventually dropped back into his customary pace, she turned to Count de Basterot to say something and found that he was not with her. She tried to turn Tommy round, but Tommy now refused either to turn *or* to stop, and firmly walked on taking not the slightest notice of Grandma's tugs on the reins, or of her cries of "Whoa, Whoa." Grandma laughed so much when she told us this story, and always maintained that Tommy understood everything that was going on and that he too was desperately bored with the endless conversation from behind him. We all thought it terribly funny a Count being up-ended by a donkey. Count de Basterot had to walk all the way home, and arrived back very hot and cross, and refused to believe that Grandma hadn't noticed that he'd fallen out when Tommy spun round so quickly!

Grandma adored the woods, and taught us such a lot about them. Every year she planted a lot of young saplings, and endlessly walked round looking at her young plantations, tearing ivy away from the older ones, and seeing that the wire netting was safely around the smaller ones to keep the rabbits away. The weather had to be very bad indeed to keep her from visiting at least the nearest seedlings. She always wore galoshes over her shoes, cotton gardening gloves over her mittens, and armed with her spud went forth daily to wage war against thistle, ivy, nettles, convolvulus and rabbits. I think one of the few times I saw her really furiously angry was when she found that several of her beautiful young larches had been cut down and taken away.

"If they'd *asked* me," she said when she got home, "I'd have given them some timber. I've never denied anyone, as they well know, and I could have taken one here and one there and thinned them out at the same time. But to go and cut ten trees from the same spot is sheer vandalism, and I hope that they will be found and punished." I had never heard her speak like this of anyone before—not even when the Black and Tans killed Malachi Quinn's young wife—shooting at everything as they drove along the road, for fear of being ambushed, they said.

Grandma certainly did give to anyone who came to the house asking for things. I can remember the streams of people out of Gort who came to ask for flowers for their church, for graves of relatives or to put in their windows when there was to be a holy procession along the streets of Gort. Grandma really liked giving for the procession best, because she said that if the flowers were in the windows of the cottages the people

93

living there would enjoy looking at them. Grandma went down to the garden with each person who came, and walked round the garden with them, making an individual bunch of mixed flowers for each one. Sometimes the flower garden looked as though there was not a single flower left in it, and yet Grandma always managed to find something blooming which, with added coloured leaves and buds, made yet another offering to the Roman Catholic Church.

I can remember my incredulity and then my fury years later when George Moore wrote saying that Grandma had tried to proselytize the Catholics of Gort. When I remember what she did to beautify their houses for the papal processions. How often and often she went out in pouring rain to get the flowers for them—often quite late in the evening when she had just sat down to her tea—and always with the one thought that if she had the flowers to give, and they wanted them, they would have all she could give. It still makes me mad to think of it. Even the Parish Priest had come once, when there was a special celebration and there had to be special flowers for the altar, and Grandma gave him every single lily out of the greenhouse, to be put on the altar of the Roman Catholic Church. If this was proselytizing, there is no doubt who gained from it.

When we were quite young, Grandma decided that we should learn the dances of our own country, and took us to have lessons at the Convent from Sister Columba. So in we all went, and Grandma sat and watched us, her foot tap-tapping to the bouncy tune of the 'Irish Washerwoman', very scratchily played on a fiddle by another Sister.

Our lessons were not an unqualified success. Sister Columba danced beautifully. She had won several prizes for her jigs and reels when she was very young, but now that she was a nun she wore long skirts, right down to the ground, and though she held them up a bit on one side, we couldn't really see her feet at all. So we never knew what steps were being danced, and all we did was to prance around, trying to guess what was going on under the long black drapes.

Every day, rain or shine, Grandma took a little bag of food down to the

94

cats in the Flower Garden. Actually it was always put in a used envelope, and sometimes the envelope was a thin miserable one and the food seeped through on to Grandma's glove, which she didn't seem to mind at all. The cats—always three of them—lived in and round the vineries to keep the rats at bay, but Grandma seemed to think that there weren't enough rats and mice to keep them happy, and daily took them their dinner, with a little jug of milk. Nu and I, who often went with her, thought that the cats had plenty of mice to eat, and when Grandma wasn't looking had a mouthful of meat or fish out of their saucers. Delicious it was too. We always wondered why the cats' food tasted so much nicer than our own food at lunch, and yet it was very strange because Grandma had put part of her own dinner into the envelope for the cats. We had seen her doing it, so we supposed that it must be the envelope which gave it that specially lovely flavour.

But it was the same with the hen food. Mary cooked a great pan full of small potatoes for the hens every day. They were turned into a couple of buckets, roughly crushed with a heavy chopper, and left to cool in the covered way to the dairy. Nu and I often ate tiny potatoes out of the bucket while they were still steaming, and they were much better than the ones we had had for our lunch. We asked Mary why they were nicer, and she said it must be the chicken meal that she mixed with the potatoes in the bucket, and we *never* had them done like this for the house.

Mary made all the butter, and sometimes let us skim the milk. It was fascinating the way the thick cream crinkled when you pushed it back from the sides of the great flat pan, it looked like corrugated paper. The pushing back part was fairly easy, but it was very difficult to get under the cream blanket without taking a lot of milk with it. On the other hand, if you broke the blanket you left lots of little islands of cream, which were much harder for Mary to fish out afterwards.

We helped with the churning too, and the thrill was terrific when we heard the change of sound from the 'splash-splash' to 'splash-plop-plop' when the butter was forming. Mary told us that butter-milk was terribly

95

good for our complexions, and that we'd be real beauties if we drank a glass. Nu tried a mouthful and was nearly sick. I—quite determined to be a beauty—drank half a glassful before thinking that there must be a pleasanter way of becoming beautiful, but deciding that I'd rather stay plain all my life, than drink more of that revolting stuff. Mary said she loved it, and drank a whole glass—our tummies turning over as we watched her.

CHAPTER XVI

Dada was a great horseman. He was killed when we were very young and
have only one visual memory of him. He was standing outside the hall
door with Mamma and Marian, and they were all taking it in turns to
wring the last drop of water out of a duster or something. I was watching
from the nursery window above, and was quite upset when Mamma fell
out of the competition early on, but then Dada and Marian went on and
on against each other, and I don't know if anyone won, because I
remember the Victoria drove up then, and Dada got into it without a
word. Marian made the sign of the cross, I remember, and Mamma just
stood and stood looking after the Victoria and I don't think she waved
and I couldn't see Dada looking back.

Dada was a terrific horseman, as well as being a very good boxer and a well-known painter, but because I was mad about horses Grandma told us stories of his riding more than anything else. One of her favourite stories was about the time he rode Sarsfield in a point-to-point, and as it was the local point-to-point everyone had backed him. Half way round Sarsfield pecked, and somehow he pulled his bridle off. Dada—knowing that all the tenants had their money on him—finished the race without a bridle, and kept Sarsfield straight on the course by using his legs, and tapping either side of his nose with his stick: he won the race too. I tried doing this on Pud, but found that Pud didn't react in the same way as Sarsfield; he merely turned round and cantered home with me shouting my head off on top. Very undignified.

Grandma also told us about the amazing 'lep' that Dada did on Sarsfield out hunting. The hounds had gone away from Roxboro' and straight over the enormous demesne wall. There was no hope of jumping it, it was far too high, and the nearest gate was some way away; Dada had got Sarsfield to jump up onto an enormous rock beside the wall, and had taken off from the top of the rock, and had landed safely in a lane on the other side. Actually, Grandma told us that Yeats had written about these things in one of the poems he wrote about Dada, and read it aloud to us.

I once rode Sarsfield long after my father was dead. Sarsfield usually lived in the Hobble field, and we often fed him with apples and sugar, and he always trotted up to the gate when we called him. One day I said to Nu that I was going to have a ride on him. Nu was quite unmoved by this suggested act of great daring. I had to get a bridle from John Diveney from the harness room because Sarsfield had a very large head and Pud's bridle wouldn't go half way up his cheek. It was quite extraordinary getting up on the old horse, who must have been about 25 years old at the time. He was miles taller than anything I'd been on before. He had a prominent and very sharp back bone, I remember, and he felt a bit awkward in his movements.

I was a little afraid that he was so old that he might fall dead with a heart attack. John had warned me not to go too fast, so I rode slowly round the Hobble field, imagining myself as Dada, and longing to gallop and see what Sarsfield really went like.

I trotted round, and turned round at the far end of the field, jogging quite slowly. Suddenly—with no warning at all—Sarsfield cocked his old ears, snorted, and broke into a strong canter. It was so sudden that I was nearly left behind, then as I collected my reins and my balance, I realised with astonishment—and I may say terror—that the old horse was heading for the great double bank in the middle of the field over which Dada schooled his horses.

Sarsfield, his ears cocked, feeling quite enormous, and enormously strong, was making straight for the bank. I can remember vividly thinking "I mustn't let him jump it, it would kill him" and also thinking "he'd jump it quite all right, but I'm sure I'd fall off" and yet longing to be like my father and jump the bank like he did ... and then at the last moment I firmly pulled Sarsfield to the right of the fence and cantered on to the end of the field.

I could feel the life go out of Sarsfield as we passed by the side of the fence. Had he thought for a moment that he was young again, and that his beloved master had been on his back? I had a sudden and overwhelming feeling of misery. John was standing by the gate and had seen what had happened.

"Could he have jumped it, John?" I asked, "Should I have let him jump it?"

John seemed to be having trouble with something in his eye, but he managed to get the fly or whatever it was out, and said:

"He might then Miss Anne, he might indeed. He was the best horse ever I saw to lep that bank, and the Master, God bless him, said he was never on a horse so clever with his feet. But—musha Miss Anne—he could have given you the divil of a fall, for 'tis a terrible long time since he lept it."

I felt I had let Sarsfield down. John had virtually said that *I* was the one that might have been hurt, and I knew that I hadn't let Sarsfield jump it because I was frightened.

I turned him round and jogged back to the far end of the field, and turned him again at the same place, waiting for the surge of memory to come again and lift his old heart. But there was no reaction at all. He jogged quietly on, taking no notice of the Bank, even though I went right up to the edge of the ditch. He never again came to life in that extraordinary way. For those few short moments I had felt what he must have been like when he was a young horse—the power and glory of movement was quite amazing—and I really felt quite dazed by it.

For some days I was very miserable, thinking that I had been awful not to let Sarsfield jump the fence, when he so obviously wanted to, and it was so *awful* the way he wasn't interested afterwards.

I told Grandma about it—I needed reassurance. Grandma never let one down. She told me that it must have been so lovely for Sarsfield to have had those few moments thinking that he was young again, and he'd known that I was part of Dada, and all his wonderful memories had flooded back for a few moments. But if he'd tried to jump the bank he was sure to have failed, stiff and old as he was, and he would have been miserable, he'd have no lovely memory, because never once—not even when he was a green young horse being schooled—never once had he fallen, and it would have been *awful* if I'd been the one to let him fall for the very first time in his life. I had done absolutely the right thing in not letting him jump the fence. Dear, dear Grandma.

CHAPTER XVII

One day Nu and I were up near the White Gate, and heard a very odd noise—a sort of loud murmur in the distance. We couldn't think what on earth it was, so we went through the White Gate, and along by the Hehir's house towards the desmesne wall. To our absolute astonishment we suddenly saw an enormous crowd of people in the park, on *our* side of the desmesne wall, and a lot of people seemed to be sitting on the wall as well.

We crept up quite close, hiding behind trees as we went, because we were rather afraid, not having seen such a lot of people together in the whole of our lives before, and we even thought that perhaps after all there were red Indians or some other tribes gathering.

We hardly dared to whisper to each other for fear of being heard, though every one was making such a lot of noise we couldn't really possibly have been, and suddenly we saw a man step up on a sort of very rough platform, made of planks supported on poles. There was a sort of roar from the crowd, and then dead silence as the man on the platform began to speak.

Nu and I looked at each other with real apprehension now. We were quite near enough to hear the man speaking, but we couldn't understand a single word he was saying. Was he really a Mohican or something? Everyone else seemed to understand him, as now and then they either shouted or cheered; the man on the platform talked and shouted and waved his arms. He was very tall and thin, and had a very white face and very black hair, and looked a little wild to us.

We got a bit bored after some time, and crept away, hiding behind trees and bushes as we went, for we weren't quite certain that we would have been welcome at this extraordinary meeting. John Diveney overtook us on the avenue, and we asked him what all those people were doing inside Coole.

"Ah," he said, "Ye shouldn't have been there at all, Miss Anne, 'twas no place for ye. 'Twas De Valera speaking to some of his lads, and sure, they knew well they'd be better off on Coole land than outside. Well they know her Ladyship wouldn't let them be took on Coole land."

It meant nothing much to us, but that evening on the landing outside the nursery, Nu and I took it in turns to be Mr De Valera addressing the crowd in incomprehensible language, and the crowd shouting and cheering. We were convulsed with laughter at our own wit, and Grandma, who came to see what on earth was going on, was delighted. She had known about the meeting, but seemed very impressed by the way we were speaking 'Irish' like De Valera. She seemed a bit surprised by what John had said to us, but she seemed quite pleased by this too.

Grandma took us to the Abbey Theatre several times. It was a major expedition from Coole. We drove to Gort Station—usually on the side car, because our luggage fitted better into the well—and caught the train there. John Diveney agitated a bit that we might miss the train; " 'Twas all right in the past" he often said, "but now that the mails travel on it ye can't trust it at all, at all. 'Tis often on time, and wouldn't wait a minyt for ye to catch it."

The Gort train took us as far as Athenry, through only two stations, Ardrahan and Craughwell. No corridors on the train, but the station-master at Gort always gave us hot water tins for our feet if it was cold.

We had to change trains at Athenry. Here it was less friendly, though of course the station master knew Grandma well, and she and he always got into deep conversation about what was going on in the countryside around. Nu and I had a wonderful time looking in all the different doors on this magnificent station. It had a separate door for the Station Master's office, a parcels office, and wonder of wonders, two doors marked respectively 'Ladies' and 'Gentlemen.' There was nothing like this at Gort, and we were very impressed.

The train journey from Athenry to The Broadstone took about three hours, and it never seemed very long. It was thrilling looking out of the windows at the country flashing past—even compared with the side car and Cobje going flat out after a large feed of corn, it was an incredible speed.

Grandma, of course, knew the journey well, as she went up to Abbey very often, and she told us about every town and most of the houses we passed.

When we got to The Broadstone, the noise and bustle was very unnerving, and we were rather overwhelmed, and clung pretty close to

Grandma, terrified that we might get separated from her, and be lost for ever in this terrible hustle and bustle. Grandma herself always seemed slightly dazed by it too, but there was always some porter who saw her at once and recognised her, and rushed up to take her bags and get a cab. Usually it was an old brougham, with a terribly thin horse drawing it. I was very upset about the thinness of the horses, and the sight of their staring coats. I was always afraid too that they would be quite incapable of pulling the cab at all, and it was always a surprise when they started off at such a terrific speed, throwing us back into the cab with a lurch. I think they soon steadied down and went quite slowly, but for about 50 or 60 yards they absolutely flew.

We always stayed at the Standard Hotel, and all the people there made a great fuss of us, knowing Grandma as well as they did, and it felt very grand going into the dining-room and being asked what we would like to eat. It was a great thrill staying in such a fine hotel. The only hotels we knew at all were Lally's and Glynn's in Gort. Lally's was half a grocer's shop, and we had never been inside either of them anyway. So we felt that we were very 'haut ton' as Grandma used to say of the Viceregal Lodge parties in the past!

Going to the Abbey with Grandma was such fun. First of all when we went into the foyer, we were taken to talk to the lady in the booking office, and then we were introduced to Mary who showed us to our places, and gave us a programme each, and hoped that we would enjoy ourselves; and then there was the thrill of the show itself. For us, who had never been inside a theatre before it was like magic. We could hardly follow anything that was going on, but it all seemed beautiful. Sally Allgood looked marvellous, and moved about like a queen, and we loved her because she sang a song to us for ourselves when we went back stage at the interval—she sang 'I know who I love, and I know who loves me' and we hoped and hoped that she would marry her 'Johnny.' We were convinced that this was a song she had written about herself and her boy.

Barry Fitzgerald was terrific, and terribly funny, and we thought he was rather like John Diveney in the way he talked, and the sort of jokes he made.

We used to go round and see some of the actors in their rooms in the interval, and were always horrified to see how badly they were made up—the lines were so obvious, and you could see all the red on their cheeks and on their mouths; and yet when the next act started they looked all right again. It seemed like more magic that they could look so completely different on stage. And their dresses too, that looked so wonderful, looked so shabby and strange close up in their rooms, that Nu and I were really rather embarrassed by the whole thing.

I think actually we really enjoyed going to the Abbey better in the mornings when there was no audience, and when all the real theatre people were about. Sean Barlow, the stage carpenter was very long-suffering, and showed us his workshop, and we saw lots of scenery he was making, and I remember being very impressed by the head he had made for Grandma's 'Dragon.'

It was rather fun too, watching Dr Larchet fiddling away in the orchestra, not dressed up at all, and counting out loud in time to the music, while the piano(s) galloped along trying to keep up with him—at least so we thought.

Lennox Robinson came in and out—rather like a ghost we thought—very very tall and thin and with a long thin nose. He didn't like us much, I don't think, and never spoke to us. Mr Yeats, if ever he appeared, just said "Good morning Anne, Good morning Catherine," and moved majestically on.

Whenever Grandma was a long time talking business with Mr Yeats and Lennox Robinson and people, Nu and I went along to Mr Millington's office. He was terribly kind to us and gave us paper and pencils and paper-clips and things to play with, and never seemed to mind how long we stayed there.

We decided once, that as we were working in a theatre and had lots of paper and two pencils each, it would be a very good idea to write a special play—just for Sally Allgood and Barry Fitzgerald to act in by themselves. Mr Millington was the only person we told, and he promised not to tell them a word about it till it was finished, and I am quite sure he never did. Actually apart from the opening scene, which was Sally Allgood standing on a rock, saying "Who is that rowing on my lake?" we didn't really get very far, because we went back to Coole the next day.

CHAPTER XVIII

Godmother lived in a house in Dominick Street, Galway, and we stayed with her for about a week once or twice a year. Godmother, who was Grandma's sister, was bed-ridden, and was either in bed or in a big armchair in the sitting-room all the time. She had a bath chair, and went out for her 'walk' every day, pulled by a man called Barnett. Barnett was a terrible looking man, dark and surly, and was deaf, or pretended to be, and whatever the weather, wore a woolly muffler and a bowler hat. Godmother shouted orders at him from her seat behind him, and he took absolutely no notice at all, so Godmother

107

leaned forward and belaboured him with her walking stick to attract his attention. Sometimes he stopped and turned round, and grunted 'Ugh?' at her, which we found terrifying, but when she told him where she wanted to go, he usually picked up the 'drawbar' and moved on in the right direction.

We went for walks with Godmother when we were staying with her, and though it was very exciting going down to the Docks, and seeing the turf boats unloading, and also the strange fish coming up in great flat baskets out of the holds, we were always a bit apprehensive for fear the dreadful Barnett did something awful, like letting Godmother run away in to the sea. Sometimes Godmother couldn't attract his attention, and then she used to tell us to go and stop him, and tell him what she wanted. We hated this, and didn't go very near him, but danced about in front of him like a couple of collie dogs trying to herd a rogue bullock. He never ever took the faintest notice of us, and in the end Godmother had to use her stick on him again. Used as we were to Coole and the great spaces and the silences of Coole, Nu and I found the whole visit rather nerve-wracking, though we were very fond of Godmother, who wrote little stories for us, and was always finding little bags of sweets hidden near her to give to us.

It was very noisy in our bedroom too; on the third floor it overlooked the street, and there were always people shouting down below and carts and sidecars going up and down, and the tram, drawn by two horses, stopped outside the house. The tram bell rang with a terrific double 'clang-clang' and the driver yelled and cursed. The street ran uphill to our left, and the horses had rather a job to get the heavy tram moving again.

There was such a lot of noise and commotion outside one evening after we had gone to bed, that Nu and I crept to the window, and were horrified to see that one of the horses had fallen down. We were in a frightful state, shivering and shivering with cold and fear that the horse would break its leg, but when they unharnessed him, he struggled to his feet, apparently quite unhurt, and stood still with his head hanging.

To our great excitement the driver came to the door of 22 and rang,

Maggie answered the door, and craning out we saw her come out a few moments later with a bucket of water. The driver—wonderful man—gave this to the horse that had fallen, and Nu and I could see from where we were, the horse's ears moving backward and forwards as he swallowed.

By this time the people inside the bus were getting very impatient, and some of them got out and came round and we could hear them shouting at the driver to hurry on as they were late already. We thought he was very brave as he took no notice at all, and let the poor horse drink as much as he wanted, and when he had finished he gave the other horse a drinkofwhat was left in the bucket, and brought the empty pail back to Maggie who was standing on the edge of the pavement.

Eventually he hitched the horses up again, the bell 'clang-clanged' and the tram moved slowly along the street and we watched it out of sight, hanging far out of the window to see it go round the corner at the top of the street. The small crowd that had stayed to see what would happen, gave a sort of small cheer, and began to drift away, and Nu and I gave a cheer too, and Maggie heard and looked up, and was furious and rushed up and ordered us back into our beds, saying we'd catch our death of cold and that she'd tell the mistress in the morning.

It was in this room in Galway that I can remember knowing that I had walked in my sleep, and I was rather frightened by it. I can remember quite vividly knowing that I had lost my umbrella, and it was absolutely essential that I find it. I searched frantically, absolutely beside myself that I couldn't find it, though I kept on thinking that I could see it, but when I came close to it, it was something else. I began to cry helplessly, sobbing as I searched, and then suddenly I began shivering, and I realised I was standing by the window in our bedroom, and not in the strange place I had been wandering around in, and the strange thing was that I was in my nightdress. By the glow of the street lights I could see that Nu was sitting up in bed staring at me.

"I was looking for my umbrella," I whispered as I climbed into bed. "I couldn't find it anywhere."

"Well, of course not," said Nu rather crossly, "You haven't got an umbrella. You are silly, and you woke me up."

She told Godmother how silly I'd been, looking all over the room, under the beds and in the cupboard, and opening all the drawers looking for my umbrella ". . . and Godmother, Anne has never had an umbrella in all her life. Wasn't she *silly*?"

Godmother told Nu that it wasn't so much that I was silly, but that I'd been sleep-walking, which made me feel immensely superior, and that Sarah—the cook—would sleep in our room every night, to make sure that I didn't walk all over the house looking in all her cupboards. Sarah was an amazing person; we really quite liked her, but she did look very odd.

She was very large indeed, with the most enormous flapping feet. She always wore men's boots, and tramped round the kitchen with great strides as though she was walking a bog, with rather bent knees. She had very long arms with enormous red hands, and had the largest mouth Nu and I had ever seen—exactly like a negro in one of our books on Geography, except that Sarah's face was very white and looked damp. She was very kind to us, and always gave us bits off what she was cooking, and though she didn't produce such luscious things as Mary did at Coole, Mary didn't like us coming into the kitchen when she was cooking.

I don't remember whether I walked again in my sleep.

Sarah's bed was put up behind a screen, so that we couldn't see her in bed, and we hardly remembered that she was there, because we were always asleep when she came to bed, and she was gone before we were awake. In fact Nu and I really believed that she didn't sleep there at all, that it was just a trick to stop me walking.

The last night before we went back to Coole we decided that we would stay awake till she came to bed to see if she really did. To keep ourselves awake we played the 'You carry on' game. One would start telling a story and go on till it got too involved and then handed it

110

over to the other who carried on till she in turn decided that her imagination was slipping, and in this way we managed to stay awake till we saw the light of a candle coming through the door, and Nu and I, pretending to be asleep, but with our eyes just open, saw the most amazing apparition come into the room.

Sarah, with her hair all tied up in bits of rag all over her head, was wearing what looked like a tent with an enormous collar. It had gigantic sleeves—or at least one gigantic sleeve, the other seemed to be rolled back, as she carried the candlestick high above her head. She really looked quite terrifying as she moved towards the screen, and I think that Nu and I might really have been very frightened but we

could hear her boots clamping on the carpet and realised that it really was Sarah.

We could see a fantastic moving shadow on the top of the wall and ceiling as she put the candle on the ground, then the thud of her boots falling on the floor, and a terrific creaking of springs as she got into bed. Then darkness as she blew out the light.

Nu and I didn't dare whisper to each other, for fear of infuriating this unknown Sarah, but I could tell from the way Nu was breathing very fast, that she was as shaken as I was myself.

On the first landing at 22 there was an enormous stuffed bear, standing on his hind legs and holding a tray in his 'hands.' He was far taller than either of us, and wasn't very attractive, though he had a terrific fascination for us, and neither of us could pass him without feeling his coat, which was very harsh to the touch, not at all soft like you'd think fur should be, and he had a sort of stuffy sooty smell, which we could smell on our hands after touching him.

He faced the stairs, and one had to go right past him to the bathroom and lav. It was all right going to our bath, because Maggie was always with us, but during the day going to the lav. on one's own was rather unnerving, and one put it off as long as possible.

It was at 22 that we heard about Dada being killed.

I can remember vividly Grandma arriving unexpectedly and looking into the sitting-room where Nu and I were, and how she never greeted us at all, just said "Where is your Mother?" and went out again. I think that Grandma not saying even "Hallo Chicks" upset us more than anything that day.

Later on Grandma came into the the sitting-room again and told me that Mamma wanted me in Godmother's room. I went in and Mamma was sitting on the Nurse's bed behind the screen in Godmother's room and she was crying and crying. It was frightening and a terrible thing to see Mamma *cry*. She usually talked a lot, and laughed and sometimes

112

got very angry, but never had I seen her crying. I had never seen any grown-up crying . . . but *Mamma*. I went up to her rather nervously.

"Grandma said you wanted me, Mamma," I said, "have you hurt yourself?"

Mamma put her arms round me for a moment.

"He loved you so much. Go back to Grandma," she said.

I hadn't a notion what was wrong, but very thankfully went back to Grandma, and asked her what was the matter with Mamma. Grandma was looking terribly stern, so we realised that something must be wrong.

"Your mother is terribly unhappy," she said in a very un-Grandma voice, "she loved your father very much, and he is dead. You must be very kind to her and try to make her happy again; and you and Nu must try and be very brave yourselves and not let your mother see you crying."

It suddenly struck me that I should be crying, that Mamma was crying and that it was expected of me too. I opened my mouth and wailed loudly. Nu, who had been building a tower with bricks, and who hadn't been listening, realised that this was a put-on wail, and joined in for fear of missing out on something.

Grandma calmed us down, and stopped us making such a hideous noise, and went out of the room and left us alone. Nu asked me at once what it had all been about, and I told her that Dada had been killed, and that Mamma was crying in Godmother's room, and Grandma had said not to let Mamma see us crying, so I cried when she wasn't there.

"Killed for ever?" Nu asked.

"I don't know," I said, "but I think it must be, as Mamma is so upset."

I think it must have been as a result of this and also hearing Sarah and Maggie talking about ships being sunk, that suddenly made me terrified that the Germans were going to come to Ireland, and I was certain that they were going to land in Galway harbour. It was a

113

terribly worrying time for me, and I kept thinking that the Germans would come and kill us all.

Maggie tried to console me by saying that the Germans would not kill anyone in Galway, that they only killed when they were crossed, and the people in Galway would be very polite and not cross them at all, and you'd not know the Germans would be in it at all, till you'd look out of the window one morning, and there they'd be driving the tram like any other Christian, and you'd only know it was them by the big steel helmet they'd be wearing.

It was agony—morning after morning—creeping to the window to see if the tram driver was wearing a big steel helmet on his head.

Once we got back to Coole, the fear faded at once. No-one could invade Coole. Coole was safe. And anyway, Grandma was there.

CHAPTER XIX

Grandma loved telling us stories about Kiltartan and Ireland which she had been told by the country people. She was wonderful at telling the stories, though usually we preferred her reading books to us. The stories she told us so often seemed perfectly normal and we couldn't see any point in them.

Grandma got a lot of stories from Curly the Piper who came to Coole at regular intervals, and sat on the seat outside the hall window for hours, while Grandma sat on the wooden chair, and listened to him talking and playing his pipes, and giving him tea and barnbrack to eat. I don't remember much of what he told her when we were very young, but later on I remember how amused Grandma was at his description of his meeting with the Princess Royal and Lord Lascelles at Portumna. The way he was let in "... and the gates locked after me, and I was able to give Lord Lascelles word of some of his relations in Co. Mayo, Knoxs and others. But 'twas the Lady was the better man of the two for she put five pounds in my hand, and I was let out through the gate and it locked after me again." Grandma adored this story, and she used to laugh and wonder what Lord Lascelles thought of news of his 'relations' being given him by Curly the Piper.

Sometimes Nu and I sat listening while Curly talked to Grandma, and I can remember once him telling Grandma that he had been ill for some time and had been in the hospital at the Workhouse for several weeks. Grandma asked him was he well looked after, and Curly said he was treated like they'd treat a lord in a big house, but that he'd never met 'fair-haired tea' till he went to the Workhouse. Grandma asked did he drink it, and Curly said he did not, till he told the nurses to "put a colour on it."

Nu and I thought this was funny, and asked Grandma later if she liked 'Anne' tea—which we thought even funnier, but Grandma always had her tea without any milk, so we never knew if she liked 'Anne' or 'Nu' tea!

Another person who talked and talked and told Grandma stories was the Basket Maker. We found him much more thrilling than Curly, because Curly obviously couldn't play his pipes while he talked, but the Basket Maker carried on weaving his baskets while telling long and involved stories to Grandma, and it was fascinating to see the baskets growing. He used to try to teach us how to make them, and though we never made anything that lasted, it was always a thrill to bend the withies in and out, even if we could never fasten the ends properly.

However, Grandma always got him to make two small baskets for Nu and me, which looked very nice, and were fun to have for a day or too, but they didn't hold many apples, and we always went back to carrying a large number of apples for our expeditions in the woods, in the elastic legs of our knickers.

The Basket Maker also made the stools we sat on for tea out of doors. Four legged stools with circular tops. They were made with yellow withies and with red dogwood, which he cut from the front lawn on the

116

way down to the flower garden. There was an enormous clump of red dogwood, and though he arrived with a great load of yellow withies, he would usually finish these on big baskets for Grandma and then he would go off with another big load, but this time all red dogwood.

When Mr Yeats was at Ballylee we went over once or twice, though I don't think we were actually appreciated there very much. Mr Yeats, of course, we knew very well as he stayed at Coole a great deal of the time, but we had hardly met Mrs Yeats till she came to live at Ballylee for holidays, and had never met the children, Michael and Anne, who were younger than Nu and me. We didn't think much of them. They lived in Dublin, and had no idea of how to behave in the country. They were much too well dressed to start with, and didn't seem to be very keen on getting wet in the stream at the foot of the castle. Michael had pointed ears and looked like the elf in Puck of Pook's Hill, and we said to him we could see fur growing on the tips of his ears and sprouting out of them. We pretended to look inside for more fur, and I filled his ears with mud, and said that all *I* could see was filth. He ran screaming into the cottage, where they lived, and I think that this was the last time we were asked over to Ballylee. I don't think we minded very much. It wasn't all that exciting, too much talk among the grown-ups and not many trees to climb and no animals. And in any case they lived in the cottage at the foot of the castle, and only Mr Yeats had a room in the castle, as it was mainly derelict, and we weren't allowed to play up and down the broken stairs; so though we were in disgrace, we were really quite pleased to be banned from further visits.

Nu and I were inveterate tree climbers. There was a terrifically high Thuya outside the flower garden and this was a wonderful tree to climb, as the branches went up nearly like a ladder. We climbed up and up till we were high above the garden wall, and could even see right down to the vineries, way over the first catalpa in the garden, which wasn't terribly high, where Tim looked very odd as he walked back and forth between them.

Grandma stopped, called to us to be careful when we shouted at her to look at us, and then she went on into the garden, carefully carrying the food for the cats in one hand and her spud in the other. We watched till she got near the vineries, and then we could see Blackie and Blackie's friends rushing out, their tails on end, running round and round her, brushing against her long skirts as she walked. We couldn't hear any sound from our great height, but we knew they'd be mewing like mad, and that Grandma would be talking to them, and telling them what she'd brought them for their dinner.

Although Grandma never seemed to be worried by how high we climbed, visitors always seemed terrified. We thought it very funny the way they clasped their hands to their mouths when they saw us, and whenever we saw Mamma we kept quiet, because she hated heights herself, and usually made us come down, because it made her knees wobble when she saw how high we were!

The first dog that I can remember at Coole was Tonks. Tonkey Boy. He was an Irish terrier, and I don't remember him as a young dog at all. He was always old in our day, and your hand smelt very strong when you patted him.

Later on I had my own dog—Taddy. Taddy was short for Tadpole. The first day I had him, a tiny little white bundle, he fell into a pond full of tadpoles, and I was certain that he was trying to catch one—he was so brave. He was a beautiful fox terrier, with one black eye and ear and his tail stuck on with a bit of black sealing wax. He was the most fantastic fighter and hunter. He was afraid of nothing.

The cats in the yard were terrified of him, knowing to their cost that he took no notice of their spits and claws and furiously arched backs. He had killed one, seizing it by the back, and giving it one tremendous shake, killing it as easily as he killed a rat. He once killed a fox, all by himself, in an earth at the far end of the Nut wood.

I was in a state because he had been out with us in the morning, but hadn't come back at lunch time, and still wasn't back by tea. I was specially afraid because he had been caught in a trap set by a poacher on the edge of the wood a few days before, and it had been a horrifying experience, as I was unable to open the jaws of the trap, and I lay beside him on the ground, trying to comfort him, and stop him biting at the trap and his foot, while Nu rushed back to the yard for help.

Listen as I could, there was no sound of screams near or far so after tea Nu and I decided that we'd go back to where we'd last remembered seeing him, near the wall into the Pond field at the far end of the Nut wood. While we were ambling along discussing him, and worrying because he was often away for the day, but always came back in time for his dinner at five, we suddenly had a nasty thought. There was a large foxes' earth near the Pond field wall, a good deal further on than we had been; perhaps he had gone down and got stuck? We looked at each other in horror. Taddy stuck underground for the whole of the day? and the men went home at six, and there'd be no one to dig him out.

I kicked and yelled at Pud and galloped on, leaving Nu and Tommy following as fast as Tommy wanted to. I made Pud go far into the wood off the path, till the bushes got too thick, and then tied him to a branch, where he could get a good feed of hazel leaves to keep him quiet, and pushed on through the undergrowth.

To my horror as I got near the earth I could hear frightful and ghastly noises coming from the hole—growlings and scufflings and terrific snorts. I couldn't see anything when I looked down the hole, but the noise was so loud that I was sure that they must be near the bend in the tunnel a couple of feet down. I rushed back to the path to wait for Nu, who must have got Tommy going very well, because she wasn't long after me, and together we went back to the earth. As we came up we could hear this awful noise again.

"Do you think he's stuck?" I said shakily, "Do you think he's being killed? . . . Taddy, Taddy," I yelled down the hole, "come out at once." The growling and snarling went on, and then suddenly Taddy's tail and rump appeared at the opening, jerking and tugging, We were terrified, thinking he was trying to escape from a fox or something that was holding him.

We bent down and seized his hind legs and pulled him clear with a great heave. Such a sight! It was awful. He was covered all over with earth, his face was unrecognisable with mud and blood, and he stank to high heaven of fox.

"Oh Taddy," we wailed, "are you all right? Are you bitten to death?"

Taddy's answer was to pant and pant, drawing in great gulps of air, but he seemed all right—not dead, and we put him down on the moss. With one plunge he was down the earth again, and before he was quite out of sight down the hole, began snarling and tugging again.

"Nu," I screamed hysterically, "I believe *he's* killed the *fox*. The fox hasn't killed him. It can only be a few feet underground."

We watched amazed as Taddy tugged and tugged, not daring to help or put our hand in in case the fox was still alive and might bite us; but Taddy didn't need our help, and as we watched he dragged the head of a fox into view. Holding it by the throat, he was dragging it into the open by inches.

It was fantastic. We had seen several foxes in the distance, mainly on the back lawn where they crept across looking for chickens, but never had we seen one so close, and it was amazing, so large—and so incredibly strong the foxy smell that we knew so well in the woods.

We just stood and stared as Taddy pulled it out. When it was about half in the open, Taddy left go, sniffed at it for a moment, gave it one half-hearted bite at the throat, and virtually fell down on his side, panting and panting. He was completely exhausted.

We examined the fox, quite fascinated. It wasn't a very pleasant sight the head end, as he and Taddy had obviously had a terrific fight before Taddy finally got him by the throat, but when we realised he was stone dead, we pulled him right out into the open, and saw he was a terrific animal, with a beautiful coat, and very large brush. He really was a large animal, and about four times the size of Taddy—who was still lying on his side, panting, his eyes half shut.

We were rather worried about Taddy, his face was a mass of blood and dirt, and he looked so terribly tired, but we carried him over the wall to the lake, and he drank and drank, and we splashed water all over him, and got a lot of the blood and mud off him.

He had a horrid gash near one eye, and both ears were horribly torn, and he seemed to be bleeding a lot from his tongue. He drank more water, and then was violently sick. We carried him back to where we had left Pud and Tommy, and I got up on Pud and Nu handed Taddy up to me, and I carried him back on Pud's back for a short way, but found this was too difficult, and put him down fairly soon. He seemed all right, apart from the fact that he trotted very slowly behind us, instead of leaping at Pud's nose and barking all the way, which was his usual habit when he was out with us.

Next day he was perfectly all right, and Mike went to find the fox, as I wanted him to cure the mask and let me have it mounted, but Mike said that the face was so torn by Taddy that it would never be any good to mount, but that he had skinned the fox, and it would make a grand rug. Mike had his own way of curing skins, which involved a great deal of salt being rubbed into them. His boots were always lined with rabbit skins that he had cured, which he wore, the furry side to his feet " 'tis no matter if you'd have a hole in your sock, the fur is fine and warm all the time." However, he had taken his boots off once when we waded across part of the lake, and the sight and smell of the skins had been revolting; so when he said he would cure the fox skin, we decided that it would probably not be very nice in the house, specially as it smelt so strong anyway, so we said he could have it himself if he wanted it. He was thrilled, and said it would make a great cover for his feet in the bed.

Pud and Taddy adored each other. Pud didn't seem to mind Taddy's endless leaping at his nose and never trod on him or took any notice at all.

When we were in Burren, Pud lived in the field in front of Mount Vernon, and he was a great one for lying down and resting himself. I have never known a pony to sit down so much. Most horses seem to stand and rest each leg in turn, but not Pud. The moment he felt weary, or had finished eating, down with him on to the ground, and without fail, Taddy then went and joined him—climbing onto his back, walking all over him, sometimes barking and barking from his perch on Pud's back, to try and annoy him, sometimes just sitting against Pud, perfectly happy to be near him. They really were the most amazing friends; and even when Pud was grazing in the field, Taddy often was with him, close to his nose, sniffing at what Pud was eating.

CHAPTER XX

The apple garden, down the lovely avenue of great lime trees on the way
to the yard, was a wonderful place in summer and early autumn. The
whole of the top walk was flanked by a wide bed of gooseberry bushes, of
many varieties, which ripened at different times—from the first yellow
hairy ones—very early rather small and very sweet, to the big red ones,
which didn't really get ripe till we were in Burren, and Grandma brought
great baskets of them to us when she came on Nu's birthday in August.

Nu and I always tackled one bush at a time, squatting on our heels,
one on either side of the bush. We'd eat gooseberry after gooseberry till
we had finished every single one. We had it absolutely taped: pick the
berry—small nip on the side to break the skin—a quick squeeze without

taking it from our mouth—and the empty skin discarded on the ground. After we had finished our bush the ground around it was completely covered in discarded skins.

Having made certain that there wasn't a single gooseberry left, we then prospected for the next most ripe bush, which was earmarked for demolition on the following day, as we weren't allowed to eat two bushes at one sitting, unless it had been attacked by birds and partially demolished before we got there. However, Grandma usually kept about ten days ahead of us, by netting ten or twelve bushes as they began to ripen. In any case, searching for the gooseberries for the morrow, meant quite a few more for to-day, as of course the only way to test ripeness was to sample each bush in turn. The skins of these 'tasters' were carefully carried in our hands, and added to the carpet of skins under the bush of the day, and if Grandma ever noticed a few red or green skins among the mass of yellow ones, she never commented on them. They really were the most heavenly fruit, and it was quite extraordinary how dull gooseberries tasted eaten off a plate, or even out of a basket, and not straight from the bush. Sometimes there were gooseberries on the table for dessert when there were visitors, and though we always ate as many as we could, looking on them as really belonging to us, we couldn't believe that they were *really* off our bushes, they were so uninteresting.

The apples were lovely too, but while we always ate gooseberries straight off the tree, we never picked the apples, only took the windfalls, of which there were plenty—and if there weren't any actually on the ground to pick up, we sometimes found ourselves 'inadvertently' pushing against a low branch, or even—almost without volition—giving it a quick shake!

We seldom ate the apples when we were in the garden, preferring to fill the legs of our knickers with them, to carry off to our camp. The elastic in our knickers usually held well, and though it wasn't particularly comfortable to have six or eight apples clustered round each leg above the knee, it was certainly the handiest way of carrying a large number.

We usually managed to transport the apples to wherever we wanted them, though if it was fairly far into the Nut wood, there were never so many when we arrived at our camp, as we ate apple after apple on our journey.

We had one rather embarrassing experience. We had collected an extra large load, and were walking slowly—legs rather apart—carrying our store of 'groceries' through the Haggart. We were actually going to do some haymaking, and realised that we'd be very thirsty, and that we'd need extra refreshment. As we walked slowly under the limes from the garden gate, Mamma and Augustus John and some lady who was staying, appeared coming up from the yard. The lady said something to Mamma, who looked closely at us, and then asked in a rather cross whisper if we had had an accident?

Rather bewildered we said "No . . . what sort of accident?" which seemed to embarrass Mamma and the lady, but made Augustus John roar with laughter. We couldn't think why he was laughing, but it seemed to annoy Mamma who then said very crossly "Well, why on earth are you walking in that odd way with your legs apart? You both look disgusting—put your legs together."

"But we can't, Mamma," we said.

"Why ever not? don't be so silly," said Mamma, looking very angry, "of course you can walk with your legs closer together. You always have up to now. Don't be so disobedient."

"But Mamma, the apples," we said. "We'll squash the apples if we do."

"Apples," said Mamma in a stunned voice, "Apples? What have apples got to do with it?"

We pulled up our short skirts and displayed our navy blue knickers, bulging all round with strange knobbly shapes.

"We always carry our apples like this," we said, "It's very handy."

Mamma was horrified.

"Disgusting," she nearly snorted, "absolutely disgusting. How can you

125

eat apples you've had in your knickers? Take them out at once and carry them properly."

One by one we took the apples out of the knees of our knickers and laid them side by side on the drive. They didn't look nearly so many as they lay there.

By this time Augustus John was rolling about screaming with laughter, which we thought was very unkind of him; and Mamma obviously thought so too, because she looked at him, and frowned, and said; "No encouragement is needed. It's not a bit funny, I find it all very depressing," and moved on towards the house.

Nu and I found that we couldn't carry more than two or three each in our hands, which was no use to us at all, and we took good care not to be seen again with apples in our pants by anyone from the house, except Grandma, of course, who didn't mind in the least.

Haymaking was great fun, though Nu and I thought it was rather hard work, and never stayed very long after we had finished whatever 'refreshment' we had brought with us.

One day though, it was terrifically exciting. We were at the gate of the Sawpit field, just going in to join the men at the far end of the field, where they were turning the hay. Suddenly we saw the hay rise up above the men in a great whirl and travel right across the field like a great swirling ghost. For a moment we thought the men were throwing it about in the air for a joke, but then we could clearly see it was travelling right past the men, and more hay rising from the ground where there was no-one, joining the mass already in the sky. We could feel no wind at all, and yet the hay was travelling quite fast, swirling as it went. It travelled over the wall into the hobble field, where the grass was close cropped and sort of vanished. We were amazed. It must have been a trick. How clever. But who on earth had done it? We went into the field and wandered towards the men, but saw them hurrying towards us. "Perhaps they're coming to show how they did it," we said to each other, "it's probably John. He's very clever at tricks and things." And we waited expectantly to hear how he'd done it. But to our amazement they didn't stop to tell us—they hurried past, making for the gate.

"Come on Miss Anne, come away quick Miss Catherine," John shouted, and he seized our hands, and took us with him, "sure the field's haunted, 'tis not safe to be in it at all. 'Tis all the fault of Johnny Hehir. Didn't he go and cut that old thorn in the corner. Sure there's no good will ever be done in the Sawpit field again," and he dropped my hand for a moment to cross himself, then caught hold of it again and hurried us out of the gate and along to the Haggart.

"Don't ye go into the field till the hay does be laid for three days" he told us, "there's no knowing what divilment would be in it," and he crossed himself again, and went off muttering to himself that Johnny might still have to pay for what he'd done.

None of the men went near the hay for nearly a week, and when they went into the field they kept crossing themselves and looking round but though Nu and I stayed watching from the gate for nearly an hour, hoping to see something exciting, nothing happened at all and we got bored and wandered off.

Some few years later though, poor Johnny Hehir got ill and was taken into Galway hospital where he died. Nu and I remembered the hay, and what we had heard John muttering under his breath, and wondered if it was from cutting the old thorn.

Nu and I spent most of our time in the woods—riding round on Pud and Tommy, making new camps, or stalking birds, seeing how close we could get to them before they flew away. We often got quite close to duck on the edge of the lake, though it was difficult the last few yards, as one had to climb over a gap in the high wall from the wood and then take cover behind the odd thorn bush.

Pigeons were our main stalking game. They sounded so sleepy with their lazy coo-coos, and we thought they would be easy to get close to, but they were really very much awake, and endlessly suspicious, and had long twisty necks so that they could turn their heads right round when

127

you were creeping up from behind, and look straight at you. They made a deafening noise as they crashed out of the tree, startling everything else in the most maddening way.

We often crawled quite close to rabbits feeding on the edge of the wood in the back lawn; though it was very strange that later on, when I had a gun, they seemed to notice me almost as soon as I started my stalk.

We only once saw a badger.

It was getting dark one evening, and it was really only the flash of its striped face we saw, as it realised we were there before we saw it, even though we were lying quite still watching some baby rabbits. Because of this we were very disbelieving when Mr Yeats came in one evening and told us all that he had been walking along in the Nut wood, and had suddenly seen a badger, which had allowed him to stroke its head before vanishing into the undergrowth.

We didn't say anything at the time, but afterwards we discussed it, and decided that either he had imagined it all—he did seem very vague quite often—or that it was Taddy he had seen, and that he hadn't recognised him in the half light. However, he himself seemed convinced that he had really stroked a badger, and later on he mentioned it in one of his poems about the woods of Coole. Nu and I were thrilled when we realised that Taddy had appeared in verse!

But we never knew if Grandma really believed his story.

She never pooh-poohed any of our stories like other grown-ups did, and sometimes we felt that though she knew they were true—she realised that they may not have been *absolutely* accurate, and we decided that Mr Yeats' story was one of these.

And I suppose—looking back—that this was a large part of the joy of living at Coole with Grandma. Knowing that whatever we said or did—however silly other people thought we were—Grandma not only understood everything we meant to do or say, she also very often made us feel even cleverer than we had thought we were ourselves.